BE A PART OF
THE PHOTOGRAPH,
NOT JUST THE
PHOTOGRAPHER

Through My Eyes— WHY TAKE THAT PHOTO?

John Madden

outskirtspress
DENVER, COLORADO

Through My Eyes - Why Take That Photo?
Be A Part Of The Photograph, Not Just The Photographer

v11.0

Outskirts Press, Inc.
http://www.outskirtspress.com

ISBN: 978-1-4787-3442-0

PRINTED IN THE UNITED STATES OF AMERICA

Book Reviews

Social media has made everyone think that a picture is a photograph. We are constantly bombarded with pictures of everyday life on Facebook and Instagram, some of which, I believe should never be shared! It isn't until you see a ***Photograph*** taken with experience, excitement and, yes love, will you be mesmerized by what was seen by the spirit and soul of the person taking that moment in time when everything was just right, the subject, the light, space, that beat of the heart in time with the "click" of the shutter.

When someone like John Madden decides to publish photographs in a book like this, he is giving you a piece of himself. In every picture, in each story, he lets you into a private part of his special world of photography. A place where he invites you to lose yourself with him as he travels to find that wonderful moment to share, to introduce you to people who you might never meet, go to places you will long to see for yourself, touch you emotionally or make you smile because he was there that day to bring you this moment in time. You see a great beauty through his eyes read a story dear to his heart that will become a favorite of yours as it has mine.

To think these are just a few of the incredible photographs Mr.

Madden has taken over the years, we can only hope that this is the first of many with the stories that accompany them that he will share with us in the future. Keep your camera clicking, Sir!

- Patricia Wallace, Corporate Trainer, Healthcare and Human Resources

. . .

The ideas, motivation and life experiences shared through the lens generate not only a sense of awe, but of peace and time. I really liked the stories behind the photos. Great work and works! John!

- John Stich, a proud scouter and Kwahadi of many years, and a lover of classic B & W photography.

. . .

I've always liked narrative writing. This book is different, eye opening and educationally well written. It takes you into the mind, of the artist eye, of John Madden. You get to learn about and be included in background, stories and facts in John's life as well as things or an event in others lives. You really don't think about what's behind photos taken, you just look at the pretty picture. But it is the inspirational story that leads to the great pictures and a good book.

- D'Aun Davis, Accountant

Contents

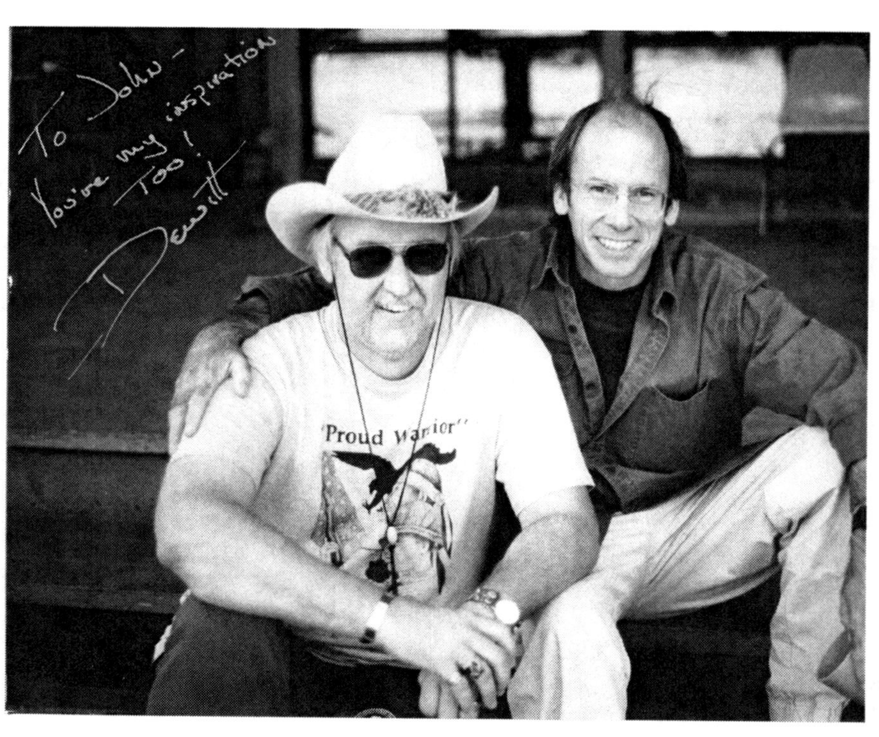
To John -
You're my inspiration
Too!
Dewitt
"Proud

Dewitt Jones

(http://www.dewittjones.com/)

For many years I've read his column in Outdoor Photography (highly recommend it) and believed "someday I'll meet and know him."

As fate would have it I was at a meeting in California, when I was in banking and walking to the lobby I saw a sign "Dewitt Jones Seminar."

I stuck my head in an open door, stood there watching and listening to him. "Yea, this was meant to be," I told myself. Have no idea if I did anything else, pick up a brochure, fill out anything or just stood there.

Years later I received an invitation to a photography workshop he was putting on at Point Reyes, California. To this date I have no idea how all this came about but it requested a bio and either photos or slides of my work. What bio, slides, or photos of what work?

I just took pictures of anything, everything and everybody. You know, I was never in the pictures as I was the one taking them.

I couldn't pass up the ego shot so I put together what I hoped was a bio along with some photos and mailed them.

> Quote: **Kudos to Dewitt Jones, a 20 year veteran photographer for National Geographic. Dewitt is one of those people who understands the power of focus; not just for a camera, but for life.**

To my totally amazement I was accepted. Figured the qualifications were very low or those wanting to go were few.

When I got there I felt like a "deer in the headlights" as all I had was a very inexpensive Minolta 35mm camera, a 50mm lens and a doubler (it doubles the focal length of you lens: i.e., a 50mm becomes a 100mm: but slows down the lens meaning it needs more light). Not exactly best image to put forward. Kind of like the country going to the city.

Remember earlier I said, "The equipment doesn't make you a professional or even a good photographer. YOU DO", but it helps! This workshop and what I observed began my awareness of and belief in that statement.

We met every morning and afternoon to talk photography, see each other's work (all work were slides developed that night and looked at the next day). It was learning not teaching as teaching goes that week. We learned from what everyone else did.

Dewitt and his beautiful lady, Lynette Sheppard, (http://www.menopausegoddessblog.com/tag/lynette- sheppard/) also took photos and showed their slides as we showed ours. No should've done this or that, why did you do what you did, but a sharing of what everyone did and why. Not questioning "why" but what did you feel and why did you take the photo?

It was a continuation of his writing in Outdoor Photography and I loved it. He was the professional photographer but his attitude was we were all the same, no one better or worse than the other. Lynette and numerous others were talented professionals in one way or another, but everyone followed Dewitt's lead, we were all equal.

Guidance was a major part of the teaching. How can I help you if you want it? Several of the participants and I have remained friends over the years, still encouraging each other. One of the most gifted photographers I've ever seen or met since then was a "Spelunker" (one who explores caves chiefly as a hobby). His work was unbelievably breathtaking and his willingness to share was extremely generous.

Two more times I was invited to participate in a photography seminar with Dewitt, Lynette, Richard A Cooke, III (rikkecook.com) and his beautiful Bronwyn (http://huiho.org/who- we- are.php) on "my island" of Molokai, Hawaii (http://visitmolokai.com/).

Those adventures are books on their own.

Molokai is 38 by 10 miles in size, no stoplights, said to be the birthplace of the Hula, the leper colony, on one end of the island there is a rain forest with unbelievable water falls, and to my Molokai is one of the most beautiful, exhilarating, enchanting, peaceful, photographical, and interesting places I've ever been.

All of which fits the Dewitt I know, as he doesn't critique he asks you and talks to you about life, the beauty of nature, capturing a moment, encourages, and enjoying what you're doing. When he talks to you you're the only person in the room. You have his undivided attention. Best type of critique there is in my humble opinion.

He talks life, Mother Nature, beauty, know yourself, believe in yourself, and is the most exhilarating mental massager you will ever meet.

Work at checking out his art, his spirit and his photography, reading him and getting to know him. You're life will be better for it. As you'll see I wrote as much about him as I did on most of the stories.

Oh yea, If you ever get a chance to go to Hawaii, go to Molokai.

> Once photography enters your bloodstream, it's like a disease
>
> - *Anonymous*

Thank you

Judy Madden, my wife for her belief, love and constant encouragement; Pride Madden Haragan, proof reading; Gene Snyder, Editor of the Denver City Press; Carolene Poole, Charles Ritchie, Harrison Madden, Susie Knutson, Mark Wilson, Dr. Gilad E. Emeil, Dr. Timothy Benton, Dr. Dustin Turner, Dr. Michael Wilkerson, Dr. Douglas Albracht, Dr. Richard Caplan; Sandy Payne for telling me years ago to write a book; Pat Wallace for proof reading and years of encouragement; Nadine Cox for telling me it's okay to write "free verse" poems and photography encouragement

Photographers: Dewitt Jones, Ansel Adams, Alfed Stilgitlz, Lynette Sheppard, Carol Robertson, Richard Cooke, Jim Goss, Jimmie Weeks, Steve Douglas,

Photographers in training: Hannah and Micah Haragan

Artists: Georgia O'Keefe, Kathy Morrow, Joe Belt, Buck Taylor, Bill Jackson, and Tatum Madden

The Why

The idea behind my book is: there are so many technical photography books but none that I know of tell the story of why the photo taken. I want people to learn how to see what others don't, to look for the banquet God (quote from Dewitt Jones) gives us everyday, to feel the photo, and to become aware of the pure fun and joy of photography.

One of my greatest photographic thrills is to have people look at me, when I'm photographing something, then look in the direction I'm photographing, look back at me and then look again, at the direction I'm photographing. Seeing the look of what is he doing? What does he see? What is the juice that fills my being?"

Or to be asked: "How long did it take you to take that photo?" Answer: "All my life!"

Or to be told: "I have a camera, I could take that photo." Reply: Great, go and do it.

This is not a technical book, it's a PHOTOGRAPHY IS FUN and every photo has a STORY.

The equipment doesn't make you a professional or even a good photographer. YOU DO!

Come on.... Go have FUN!

"...One sees differently with color photography than black-and- white... in short, visualization must be modified by the specific nature of the equipment and materials being used."

- Ansel Adams

CHAPTER 1

People

People have always been a fascinating subject matter for me. I mean look at it, no matter who, they're all different yet the same. For years, I've scoped out a crowd to find someone who "stands out." Not height wise, but character wise. A normal individual, who's anything but normal and to some, may appear a little edgy. An independent person but not necessarily a loner, a thinker, a one- of- a- kind, a person people are drawn to, and someone who lights up the room when they walk in. By that I mean someone I'd like to meet, visit with, and find out more about through my camera lens.

I'm better at lens introductions and small talk than person- to- person. It a curse artistic people have.

Oh, just thought of one of my favorite people photos. I was an exhibitor at Michael Martin Murphy's West Fest at Copper Mountain, Colorado with a back stage pass.

Out comes one of my true music heroes John Denver. I'm less than 10 feet from him and.... well that's for another books on faces. Watch for it. It'll be fun.

"Every single thing that has ever happened in your life is preparing you for a moment that is yet to come."

- Unknown

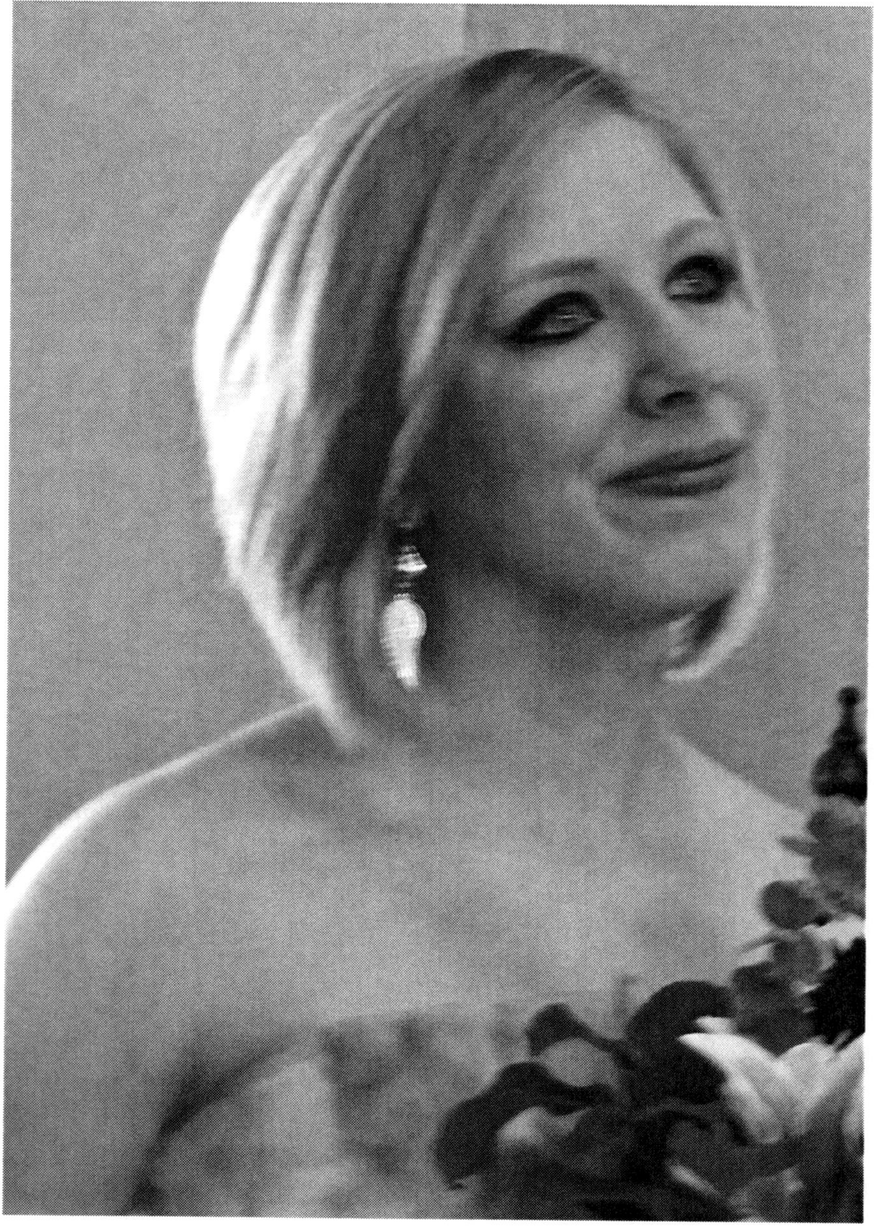

Standing behind her sister, Kate reminded me of a scene from the 1997 movie "Fairy Tale - A True Story." She was wrapped in a softness, happiness, and love for her sister and her wedding, that said— "soft focus."

Kathryn (Kate) Christine Carroll

Her sister's wedding was in the country, in a beautiful home of friends. The friends had built it themselves. It's a split level with the laundry in the basement along with everything needed to can vegetables and bottle wine from their grapes.

It was an enjoyable experience just to walk through the house. On top of that it had been decorated with the most unusual items. An old phonograph, old phone, candy cigars and cigarettes, old typewriter, very old post cards, Bit- O- Honey candy, hand made chocolate candy, iced down Old Dr Pepper bottles with Dr Pepper in them, old books, an old desk, fishing tackle and toys, old roller skates, old dial phone, lots of crystal bottles with a wide variety of things in them and all adorned with lace, old clock, more flowers than most flower gardens have, bags of fresh popcorn, a popcorn machine, old baskets, very old adding machine, old Polaroid camera, photo albums with old photos, bottles of water and of course beer all iced down in an old wheel barrel.

Upbeat and happy signs such as: "Never miss a chance to Dance" – "You look marvelous now get out there and Dance" – "When ever I see your Smiling Face I have to Smile Myself because I love YOU Yes I Do."

It was without a doubt the most enjoyable, relaxed, fun filled with unbelievable food wedding I've ever been to.

The bride was not old by any means but she had a love for old things and her beauty, smile and happiness filled the house with a magical aurora.

Her family is the most loving, close, caring, and honesty happy family. Mom and Dad started the walk down the aisle dancing together. As did all grandparents, bridesmaid, bridegroom and even the preacher.

Sitting there, taking it all in, smiling from ear to ear I notice the bridesmaid, her sister. Kate is one of the most beautiful inside and outside young ladies anyone would ever have the opportunity to meet and know.

As if I were a robot, I raised my camera and zoomed in. Standing behind her sister, Kate reminded me of a scene from the 1997 movie "Fairy Tale - A True Story." She was wrapped in a softness, happiness, and love for her sister and her wedding, that said—"soft focus." I captured it.

"The best part of beauty is that which no picture can express."

- Francis Bacon

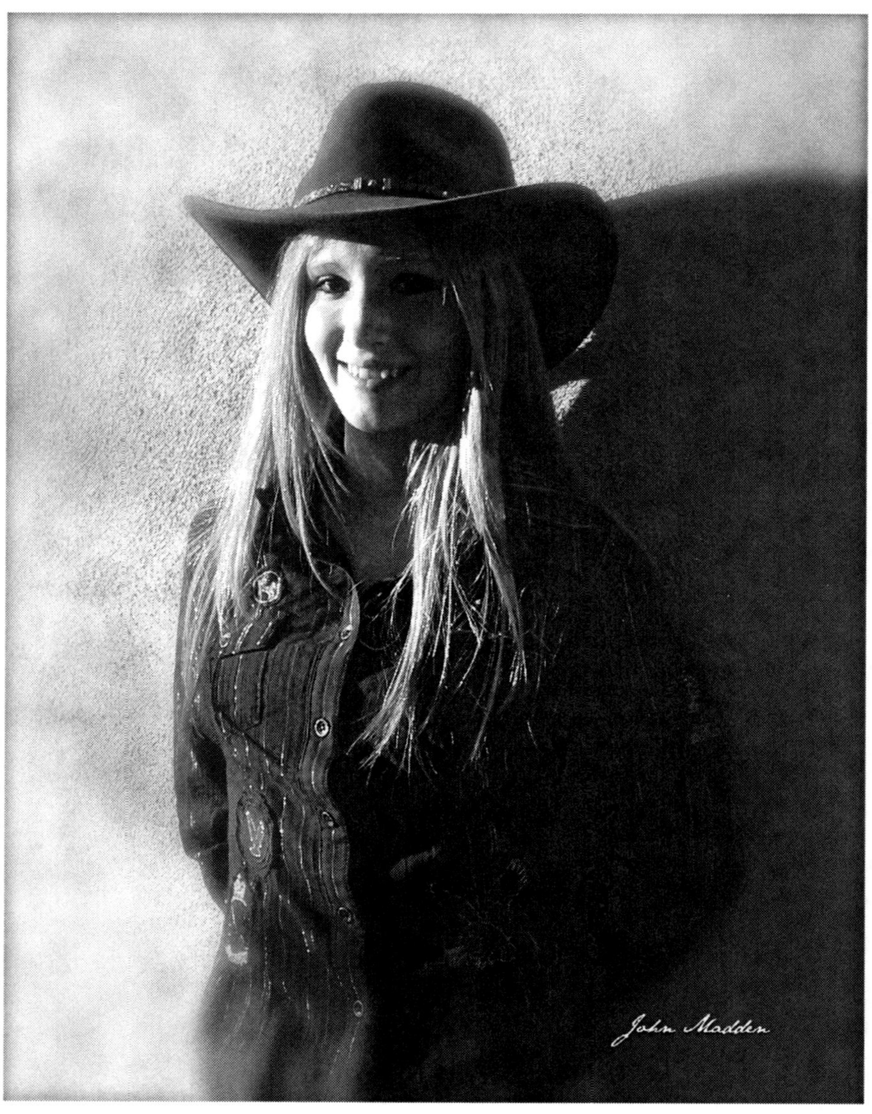
John Madden

Meridith Ann Carroll Stubblefield

Meridith was on a "Lets see New Mexico" trip with her parents, an uncle and aunt, a cousin and his wife in Albuquerque, NM at Old Town. Old Town is very historical and goes back to when the Spanish founded the city in 1706.

It's around ten blocks of adobe buildings that have become souvenir shops, places to eat, (check out La Hacienda restaurant), San Felipe de Neri Church, art shops, jewelers, and a sheltered central plaza. The New Mexico phrase "Manna" (tomorrow) engulfs the atmosphere and has a tendency to slow down and relax all who visit there.

Photographically, it's alive with subjects on steroids. Everywhere you look there's a photograph worth your attention and camera. It might be people, buildings, art, odd objects, animals, or trees. You can overload yourself with pleasurable subject matter.

Leaning up against an adobe building, Meredith stood out like lighthouse in a storm. All the history and beauty of Old Town, the shops, vendors, and the plaza paled compared to her striking beauty and naturalness.

Raise camera, focus, horizontal, vertical, and click, click.

WOW!

Love no- brainers.

> "Don't you dare, for one more second, surround yourself with people who are not aware of the greatness that you are."
>
> \- Jo Blackwell- Preston

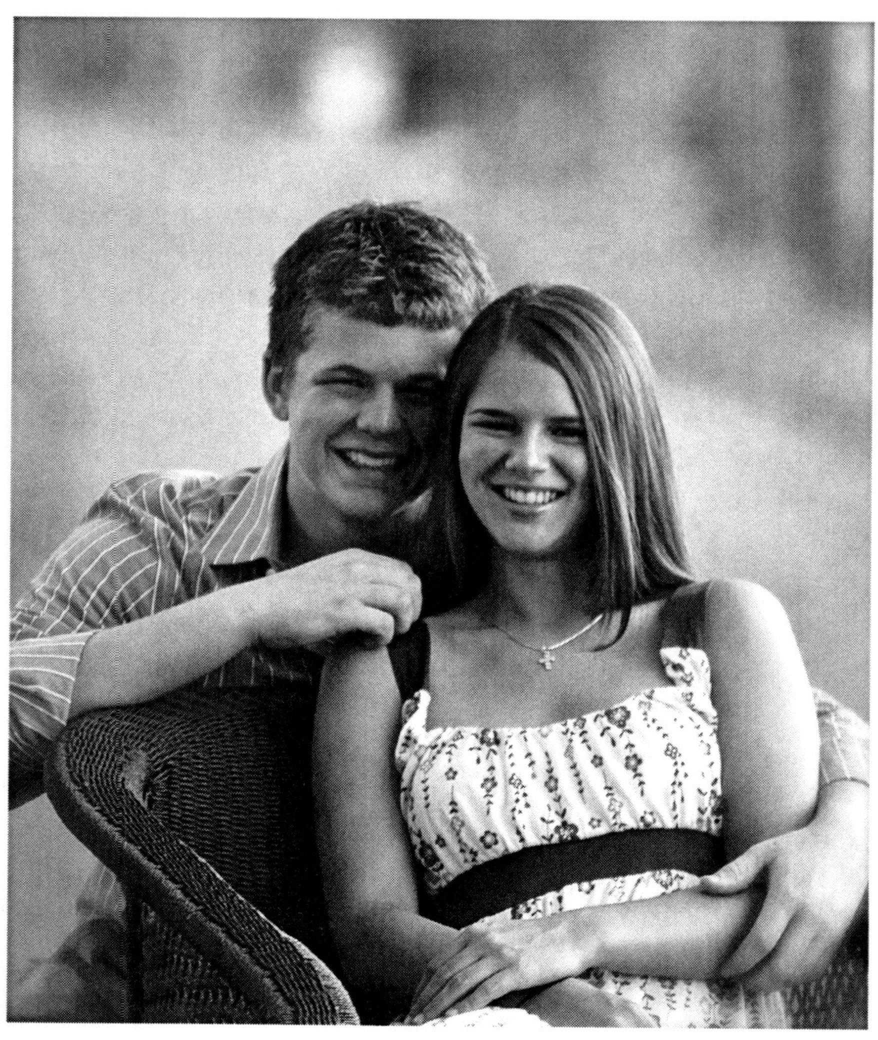

Joshua and Brett

My nephew, Joshua Smith and his beautiful girlfriend Brett Lindsay were sophomores in high school and had just started dating when this was taken. Both had the heavy weight of being good looking, very friendly, well liked, smart, and loaded with personality.

They didn't get all that from me but from their parents. Genetics! I've never understood how all that can skip some generations.

Years later they married, went to the University of Mississippi, "Ole Miss."

Josh's family, my dear sister Linda Candease (I call her Missy) Smith lived in Madison, Mississippi. In front of their house was a long single lane tree lined road, the kind of trees that hang over and protect a road as if they are road tree guardians.

It's an old romantic of a hundred years ago Southern path that's been covered with asphalt. At least that's the way I see and vision it.

We were taking their photos all around the house, barn, fences, and the road. I don't remember whose idea it was of getting a chair, putting it in the road, and having them sit and/or stand on it.

I had an idea and wanted to see what it looked like so:

* Okay Josh, sit in the chair and Brett stand behind him.
* No change places.
* No move the chair and just touch the chair.
* No stand beside each other.
* No can you both sit in the chair?
* No I don't think standing in the chair, together or singular is a good idea.

* No Brett stand beside the chair and Josh have a seat.
* No change places.

After an unknown number of "No" and wearing everyone out came, I heard myself say.

*Brett please sit in the chair, Josh get behind her and kneel down.

Oh YEA, that's it.... smile, even if it hurts after hours, smile, click, click, click, and one more for good luck.

Cool.... that's a WOW!

Question to myself: Why did it take so long for you to get it right?

Best answer at the time to self: At times it's so hard to be creative, to make it look and feel just right, and this day was one of those times.

Today they are: Both graduated from Ole Miss with honors.

Brett Lindsey Smith, has her PharmD (doctor of pharmacy) and Joshua Ryan Smith, is going to the University of Mississippi Medical Center to become a doctor (an MD) all because I took this great photo of them.

Tis a burden I do my best to carry.

"The first time I sang in church; two hundred people changed their religion."

- Fred Allen

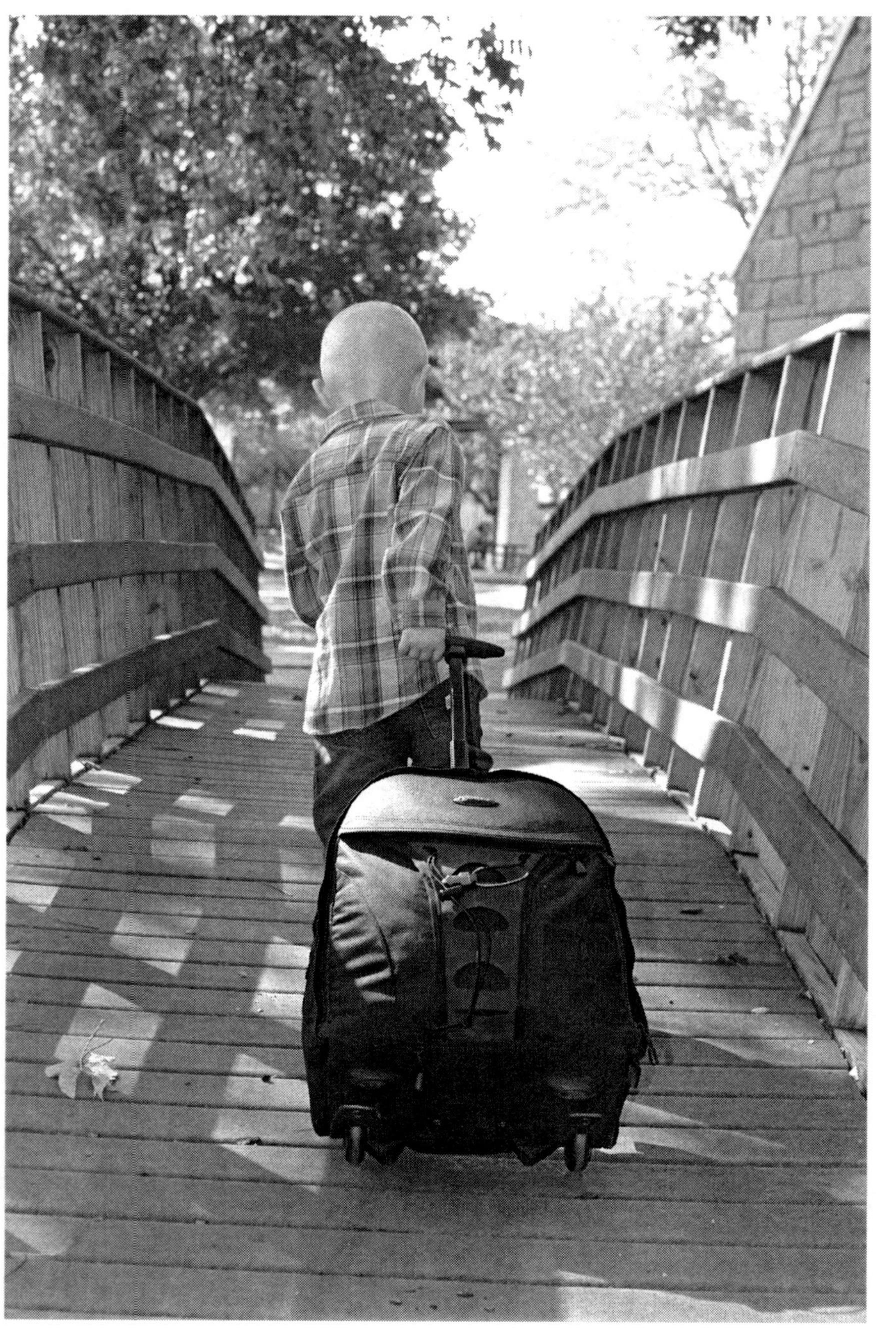

Harrison

After taking Christmas card photos and heading back to the car, my grandson, Harrison, wanted to pull my camera bag.

He's very confident and self assured, so even though I thought the bag might be to much, he wanted to pull "Pops' camera bag.

Don't know about you, but this Pops very seldom disagrees with grandchildren. After all it's in the "Grandparent- Grandchildren" book. Spoil them and let their parents sort it out and deal with it. Isn't it karma for how they acted growing up?

You know "the older the parents get the smarter their parents were/ are." I could give you a list of things it's all right for grandchildren to do but not their parents growing up.

NO WAY!

It's surprising how many times when you go with it, so to speak, and no one gets in trouble for it, that something wonderful happens.

I didn't get scolded, for letting him pull my camera bag, by his parents, family, or anyone and this wonderful photo was my reward.

That's a real win- win.

"Baseball is like church. Many attend few understand."
- Leo Durocer

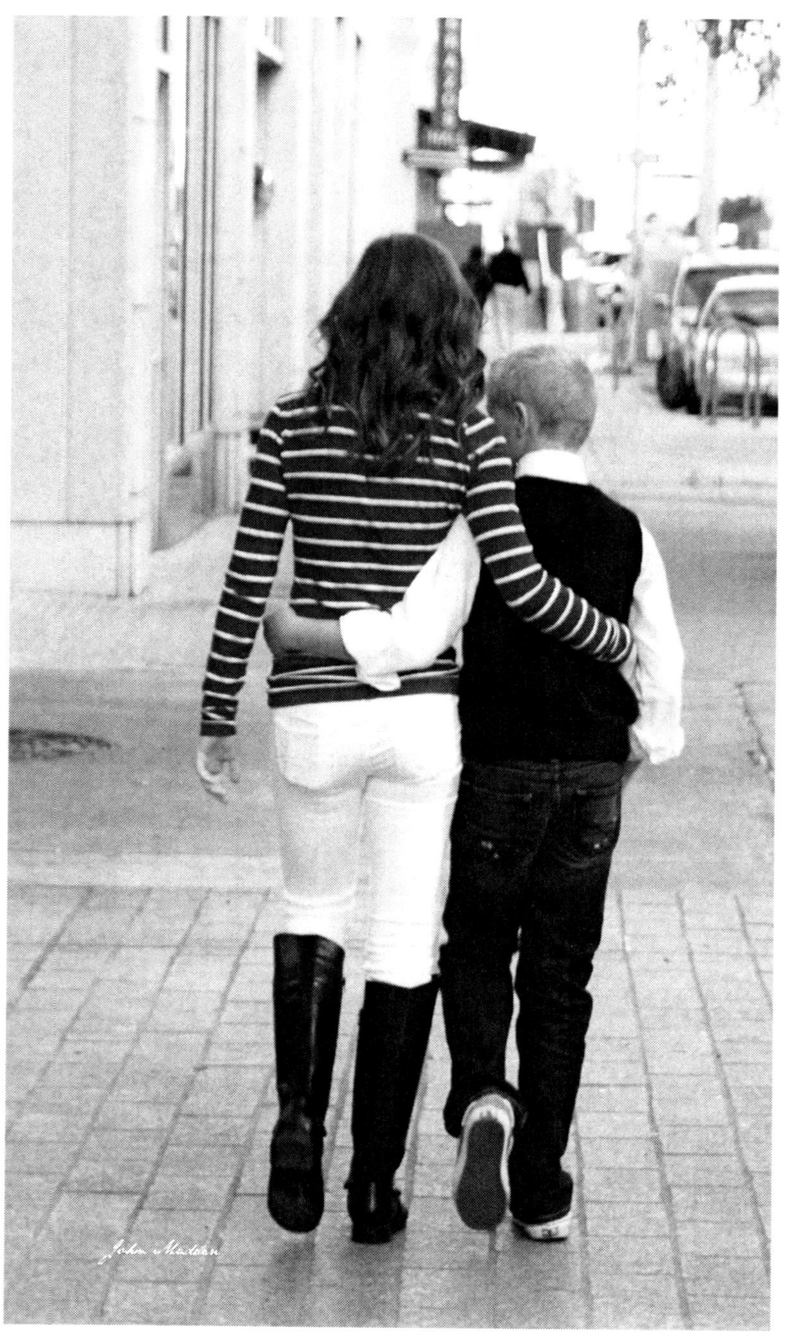

Tatum (T) and Harrison (H)

Thanksgiving 2013 we had the opportunity to share the day, in Leander, Texas with my son, his beautiful wife, my daughter and their four youngins-our grandchildren. Nothing beats being with grandchildren.

Dad, me, being a photographer had the requested pleasure of taking photos for Christmas cards. Downtown Austin, Texas was our photo studio and we made the most of it. There's a sign, on a building, saying, "Welcome to Austin." The sign is famous, however the building seems to be there to maintain the sign. The sign covers the entire south wall of the building, on a narrow street, with a stoplight, and lots of foot traffic. We did it and moved on.

The Texas state capital has twenty- five to 27 old, eloquent shaped trees, surrounding it as if being guardians of Texas history. In fact they're called the "Trail of Trees." The native pecan tree (Carya ill-noensis) became the official tree of Texas in 1919. We climbed up, sat on, sat in, and stood by, around and behind one of the most picturesque pecan trees.

It had character and branches that beckoned, no screamed out, climb me, climb me! I did my utmost to accommodate it by asking my family to do just that, climb all over it.

Wait, I'm all out of adjustment and focus here. That's no way for a photographer to be.

The tree's not what I have included. I got carried away with the memory.

Earlier we were walking down Third Street to Congress Avenue where there was a big guitar. That's one of the photos the kids wanted. After taking a dozen or so photos, we ambled back down Third Street. In `case you don't know about 6th street in Austin it's historical and the entertainment district of Austin.

Anyway, everyone was grouped together, talking, laughing and suddenly the group split, for a moment and I saw WOW.

As my friend DeWitt Jones says "Mother Nature provides us a banquet every day, we just have to look up."

In this case Mother Nature was trumped by "natural" as T and H are naturally together, supporting each other, best friends, and it's a wonderful thing to see.

I'm pleased and proud to share them with you.

Sometimes being lucky is better than being good and this case I was in the right place at the right time.

"If you see something that moves you, and then snap it, you keep a moment."

- *Linda McCartney*

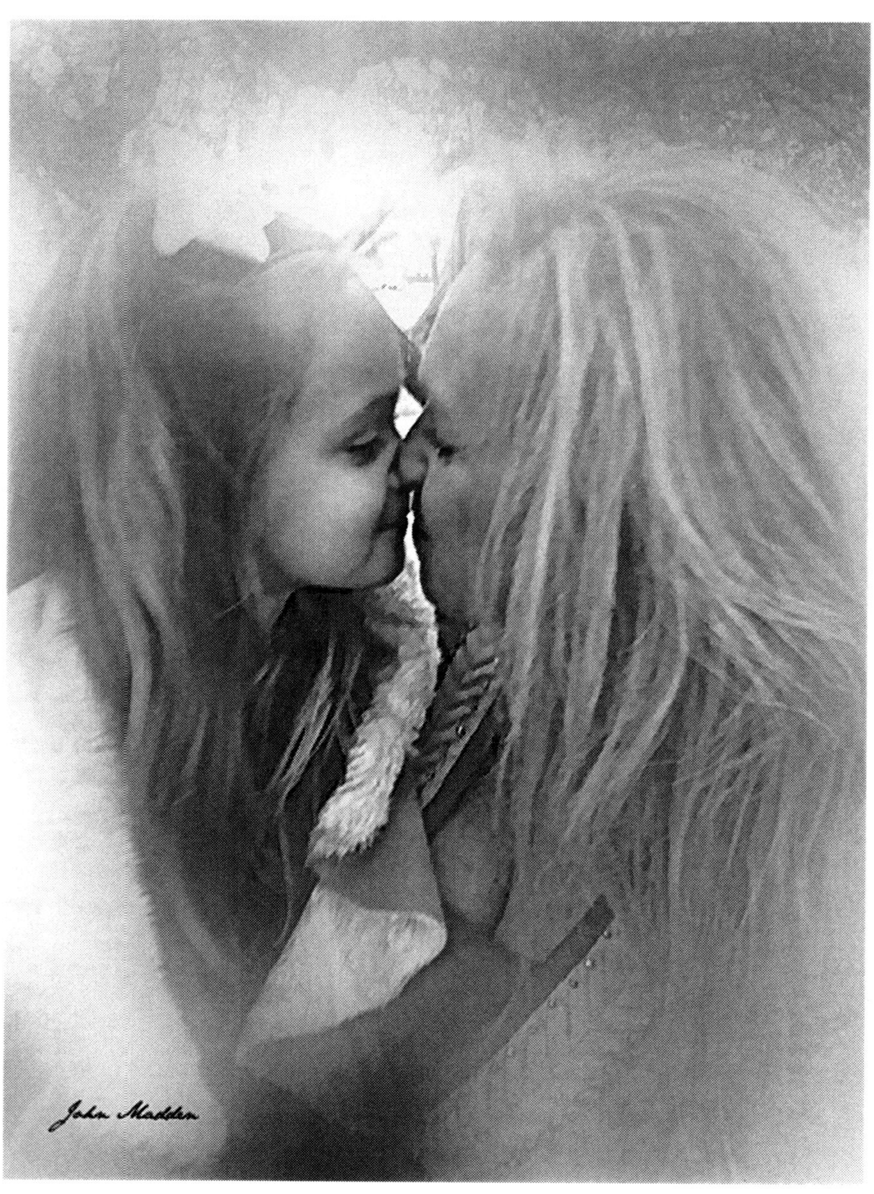
John Madden

Jennifer and daughter, Jessica

Thanksgiving 2013 we were in Leander, Texas for the holiday and to photograph our oldest son, Shawn, and his family for Christmas cards.

On the one day, we had, it was late when we finished. Some time during a long day of photography, Shawn, mentions his friend was wondering if I'd have time to do the same for his family?

We met them at the park where I had previously, photographed Shawn's family. There were lots of trees, a playground, and lots of lawn. So photo possibilities were everywhere.

Going to a group of characteristically grown trees with low hanging branches, we began. One tree in particular had a long and low hanging branch that could be sat on, stood in front or behind of, and easy to group people around.

After numerous shots of the Dad and son, Mom and daughter, kids, and all the family, I noticed the sun dropping in the West and had this idea.

I asked Mom and daughter to stand in such a way that the glow of the sun formed a halo behind and between them. Without asking they leaned in and kissed each other on their cheeks.

Do that again I said with excitement. Not risking missing the moment I took numerous photos as fast as I could. It was such an innocence and loving moment I wanted to make sure I got it, all of it.

Learning to pay close attention, seeing what Mother Nature adds or allows for you, seeing what others don't see, and believing can provide you with the most extraordinary photos.

> "Smiling is definitely one of the best beauty remedies. If you have a good sense of humor and a good approach to life, that's beautiful."
>
> - Rashida Jones

CHAPTER **2**

Southwest

The **Kwahadi Dancers** (www.kwahadi.com) have been around since 1944. Over 1,800 scouts have been Kwahadis. Every summer they take a tour that includes many states within the United States. Every fifth year they take a tour of Europe.

1985 Jordan
1999 Germany
2004 Hawaii
2009 UK and Ireland
2014 Italy, France, and UK
2019 ???

I've been in the Boy Scouts of America since I was eight and several years ago I moved to Amarillo, Texas just so I could finally be a Kwahadi. The Kwahadi Dancers are the best keep secret in Amarillo.

Since 1944: 300 have earned the rank of Eagle (BSA) and the Gold Award (GSA)

My wife, Judy, and I are Cherokee by heritage; we go to Pow Wows and dance, put on presentation for schools, groups, and Texas State Parks.

Of course I take my camera. A Pow Wow is like a big family reunion with sacred traditions woven through all life as well as the Pow Wow, a grand entry, dance contests, arts and crafts, the most beautiful regalia (what we wear, not a costume) which is different for each dance style, and the little tykes (the children)! You have to come and see to enjoy the celebration, fun, visiting, families, and an opportunity to see "We are all one people," We dance in a circle, like the circle of life, always in a clockwise direction.

FYI: Bring your own chairs and google:
http://www.powwows.com/pow- wow- etiquette/

We also have a foundation 4Directions, Inc. through which we have an annual **FREE CLOTHES** give- away to Native American individuals and reservations. In seven years we've helped over 6,700 people from over 50 tribes.

Our long- term goal is to provide scholarships to Native American youth to assist in living in two cultures.

Check us out at:

www.facebook/fourdirectiosinc

http://fourdirections- helping- hands.blogspot

Being a **Native American** how could I not also be into cowboys? Well actually deeper than that. I grew up in South Dakota and it's all about Cowboys and Indians. I also grew up in New Mexico and it's full of Indians, Cowboys, and Cowgirls.

When I was at Eastern New Mexico University (ENMU), in Portales, New Mexico (I was on the 9 year to graduate program) working full time while going to classes on my lunch hour and at night, plus cowboying at the feedlot on Saturday and Sunday- it was my job to drive in to town to give out the night deposit bags at 8 AM on Saturday. By then I had been riding the pins, working and feeding cattle since 4AM. So to say I smelled was an understatement.

I know you'll find this hard to believe, but I enjoyed going to the bank, spurs, smelly chaps, cattle n horse poop attached to me, smell of the grain and the perfume from the feedlot, when I meet the people who were use to seeing me in a suit/sports coat and slacks and watching them endure.

Figured if I had been up since 3:30AM to get to work, then have to give them their bags at 8AM!

They needed my help to walk away totally awake!

I've always been a **rodeo junkie**. Not a participant but a rodeo photographer junkie. The men and women who rodeo are some of the most gifted athletics and if you have a chance to go see them, DO.

Amarillo is the home of the Working Ranch Cowboy Association (http://wrca.org). The difference with most rodeos is they're professional cowboys competing for ranking and money to bigger $ rodeos.

The WRCA are real, working on a ranch and do it everyday cowboys and cowgirls as a lifestyle. They're the toughest and hardest folks you've ever seen.

I've been fortunate to have a press pass for several WRCA rodeos and it's 100% fun, hard work, and wonderment. How do they do that?

"The wind whips through the canyons of the American Southwest, and there is no one to hear it but us - a reminder of the 40,000 generations of thinking men and women who preceded us, about whom we know almost nothing, upon whom our civilization is based."

- Dr. Carl Sagan

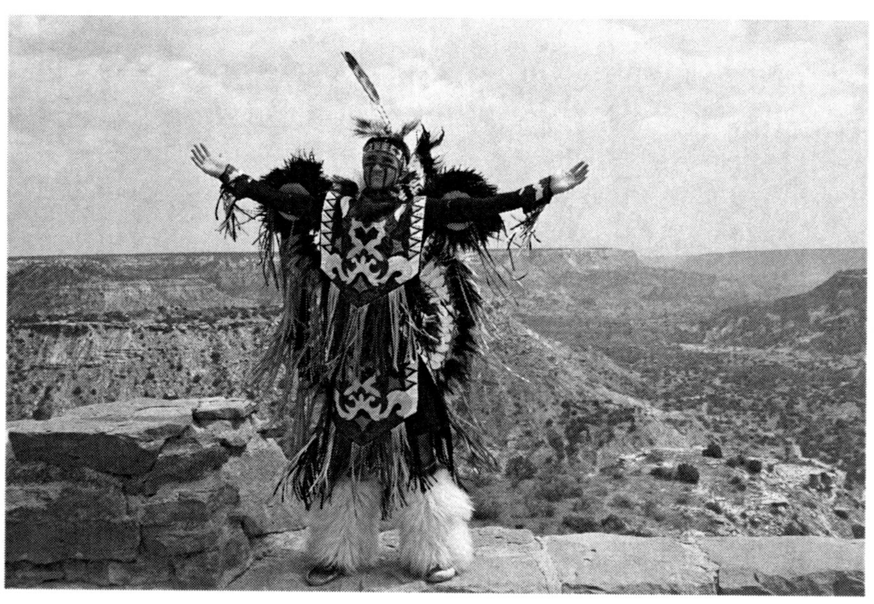

Nick Wilson

Nick is a Kwahadi Dancer (Kwahadi.com) who began as a young boy and was elected to Chief twice by his peers.

As previously mentioned I'm a long time Pow Wow goer and Gourd Dancer. That being said, I've seen hundreds of dancers, especially fast dancers such as Nick. Like David Sanders, Nick isn't Native American but dances to honor, respect, and proudly represent Native American dances and dancers.

He's extremely talented and exemplifies, to the best of his ability and knowledge, the standards of a "Fancy Dancer." Also referred to as the "Fancy War Dance."

He's one of my favorite Kwahadi Dancers to watch. He's very dramatic and just watching him dance makes me physically tired.

It's a young man's dance, however there is a Comanche dancer named "Blocks The Sun" and he does, that is a Fancy Dancer. He's a BIG man and moves as fast as a deer.

Nick and I were at Palo Duro Canyon State Park: (http://www.tpwd.state.tx.us/state- parks/palo- duro- canyon) near Canyon, Texas for a photo shoot. It's called "The Grand Canyon of Texas." It's beautiful, historical, and assessable by vehicle, horseback, motorcycle, foot and bicycle.

It was the winter home for many Native American tribes, including the Comanche's, lead by Quanah Parker, Kiowa, and Apaches to name a few.

In 1934 the Civilian Conservation Corps built a rough road, into the canyon, and it's well documented in the museum and museum store.

With all the history, we found many places and things to photograph with and around. It was a fun day. That plus Nick's regalia is so outstanding and with all his years of dancing he has a good grasp on how to present the energy, strength, and performance of a Fancy Dancer.

He represents the Kwahadi's, high ceremonial dance standards of Native American dancers, and the youth of today. He's also an Eagle Scout and is currently enrolled in college in Colorado working toward a degree.

Feel the drama, strength, and pride he embodies. That my friend is the joy of photography that's there for you to capture and enjoy.

"This nation will remain the land of the free only so long as it is the home of the brave."

- Elmer Davis

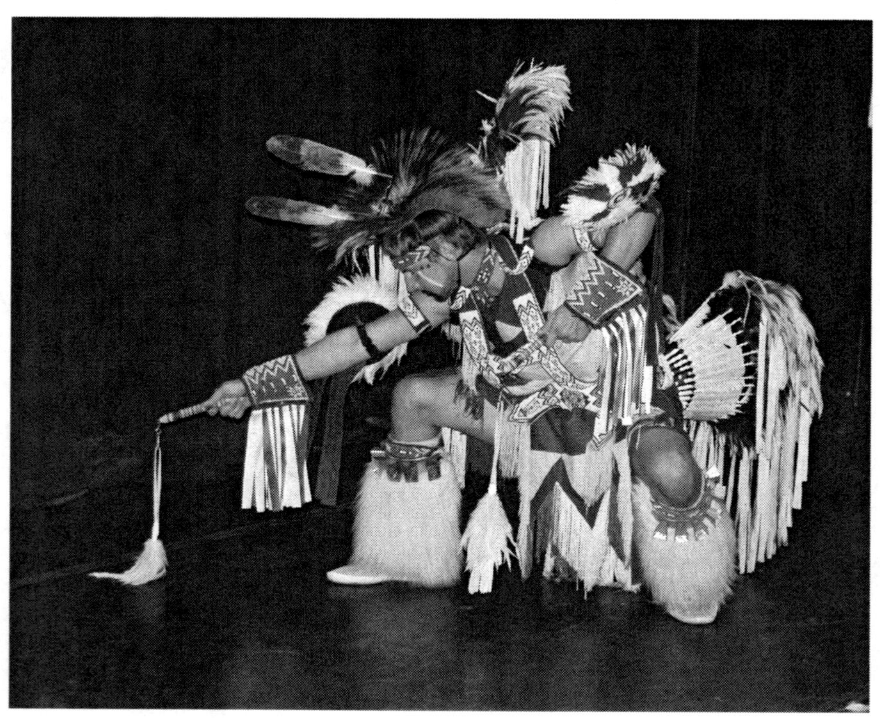

David Sanders

David is a Kwahadi Dancer (www.kwahadi.com), which is a Venture Crew under the BSA (Boy Scouts of America). A Venture crew can be co-ed, ages from thirteen and 21 years old. They're area of interests range from medical, law enforcement, and high adventure, to any number of areas.

The Kwahadis were on a European tour including: Ireland, Northern Ireland, Scotland, England, and Paris, in 2009. They put on Native American dances. Actually it's a "we" as I'm an associate advisor and singer.

Eighteen shows in twenty- one days with dances included a wide variety of Native American dances. David is dressed as a "Fancy Dancer" sometimes referred to as the Fancy War Dance. The dancers are usually very young, athletic, and dance extremely fast dance.

It's rumored to come from the Ponca Tribe sometime between 1920-1930 to help maintain their culture and religion. Their regalia are very colorful, and often the design comes from family members.

David is also an Associate Advisor in addition to having grown up in the Kwahadi program from beginning dancer to Head Chief (the youth leader). He's the track coach at a local high school and married.

I've been going to and dancing at Pow Wows for many years David, while not being Native American himself, is one of the best Fancy Dancers around. He's dedicated, skilled, and works to represent and present the Native Americans and their dances with respect and pride in his dancing.

This move, at the end of his dance, is like his signature. It's very dramatic and whomever he ends in front of is thrilled and usually slides back. He smiles at them and with that the roar of applause fills the room.

"I don't travel and tell stories, because that's not the way these days. But I write my books to be read aloud, and I think of myself in that oral tradition."

- Louis L'Amour

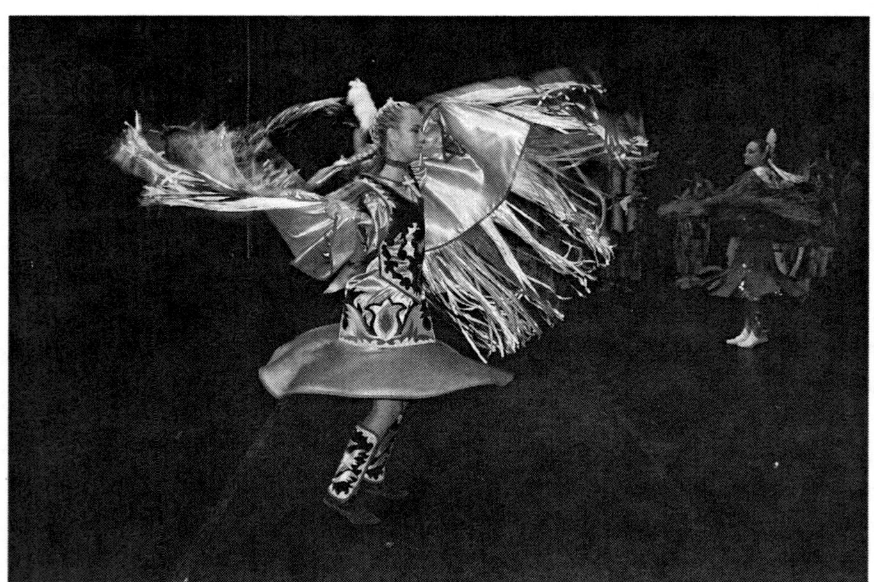

Lauren Russell and Katy Silor Shawl Dancers

Think of a butterfly in flight with elaborate designs on its wings, with ribbons in tune with the wings, keeping in time with the drum, and you have a shawl dancer.

It's the newest of the Native American Pow Wow dances and often called the Northern Shawl as the dance came from the Northern Tribes.

The colors are very bright, beautiful, and colorful embracing butterflies. The dancers wear their shawls on their shoulders, spinning and jumping around to the music of the drum. Their dance is graceful, poetic, and at the same time light as a feather.

The shawls have delicate designs, ribbon works, and long fringe at the end of the shawl, all which add to the vision of a butterfly floating on the wind or searching nectar.

With numerous shawl dancers dancing together it's pure poetry in motion as well as a rainbow of color.

Both of these shawl dancers, Lauren Russell and Katy Silor are members of the, Kwoneshi dancers (female) of the Kwahadi Dancers (Kwahadi.com).

> "Shawl dancers imitate butterflies in flight."
>
> - Unknown

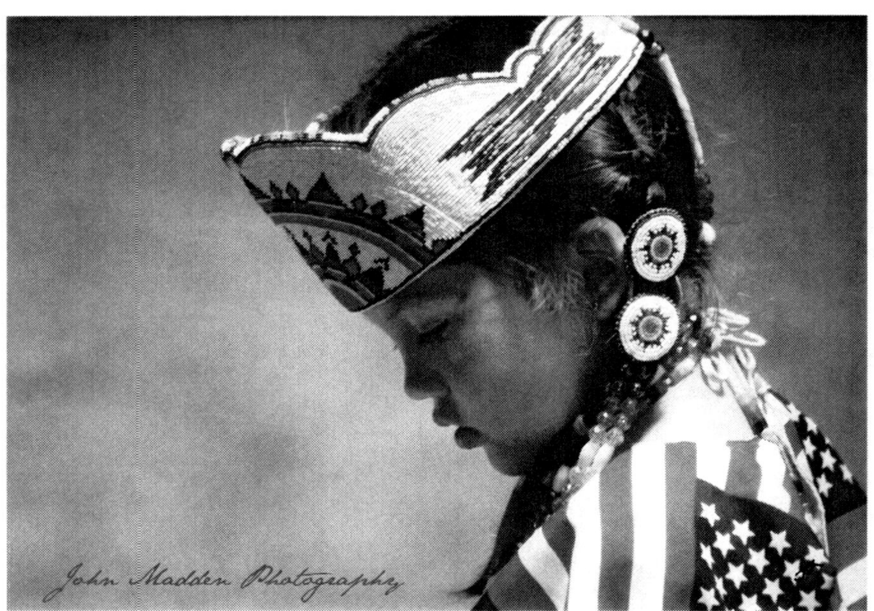
John Madden Photography

Comanche Princess

Being a Gourd Dancer, Pow Wows are like a spiritual injection of life. What are a Pow Wow and a Gourd Dancer you ask?

A Pow Wow is a gathering of Native Americans to dance, visit, sing, renew friendships, laugh, eat, watch contest dancing, celebrate their customs and heritage, honor their elders and ancestors, and share the culture with others. It's honoring America, Native American tribes, respected societies, honoring all veterans, first responders, and all who have given their all.

It's a time for non Native Americans to learn, photograph, watch, and enjoy the pageantry, color and pride of a rich culture and it's people.

A Gourd dance is not a traditional Pow Wow dance, such as Men's Traditional, Men's Grass, Men's Fancy, Women's Traditional, Women's Jingle, and Women's Fancy or Shawl, Round, and Intertribal dances.

The Gourd Dance is a man's dance, believed to have started with the Kiowa as the dance of the Tis- pe- go warrior society. The modern name comes from the rattle used, often a gourd, on a handle, with something inside to make the rattle sound.

Now a days the dancers are usually veteran, veterans family, friends and in some cases first responders and those so honored for putting their life on the line for others.

If there is a Gourd Dance at a Pow Wow is happens before anything else. It's a "blessing/cleansing" of the arena. Think of it as prayers being offered up for all in attendance and participating as well as ancestors and God. There is a drum (thought of as the heartbeat of

Mother Earth) in the center of the arena that singers sit around, beat with their personal drumsticks, and sing.

The dancers are in a large circle outside the drum and as the singers sing, either dance towards the drum or around it, usually in a clockwise rotation. At different beats of a Gourd song, they move forward, stop, drop their head then raise it, and continue moving till that song stops. Then they move back to where they started and start over on the next song.

It's a wonderful time and an honor to be dancing with such a variety of men, young men, and boys in the circle. Women dance, in place, just inside the circle, behind the dancers. They're honoring and supporting the Gourd Dancers and historical societies they belong to.

At a Pow Wow in Fort Worth, Texas at the famous Stockyard Coliseum and during an Intertribal dance everyone, including audience participants, will and can dance. Women should wear a shawl if not in regalia. Regalia are what the dancers are wearing. It has history, tradition, and often- family colors. It's not a "costume."

Looking up, to the Intertribal dance, there she was. A young Comanche Princes. Wow!

Isn't she beautiful?

Stay alert and that daily bouquet will be there.... you just have to look up.

"Remember that your children are not your own, but are lent to you by the Creator."

- Native American Proverb Quote

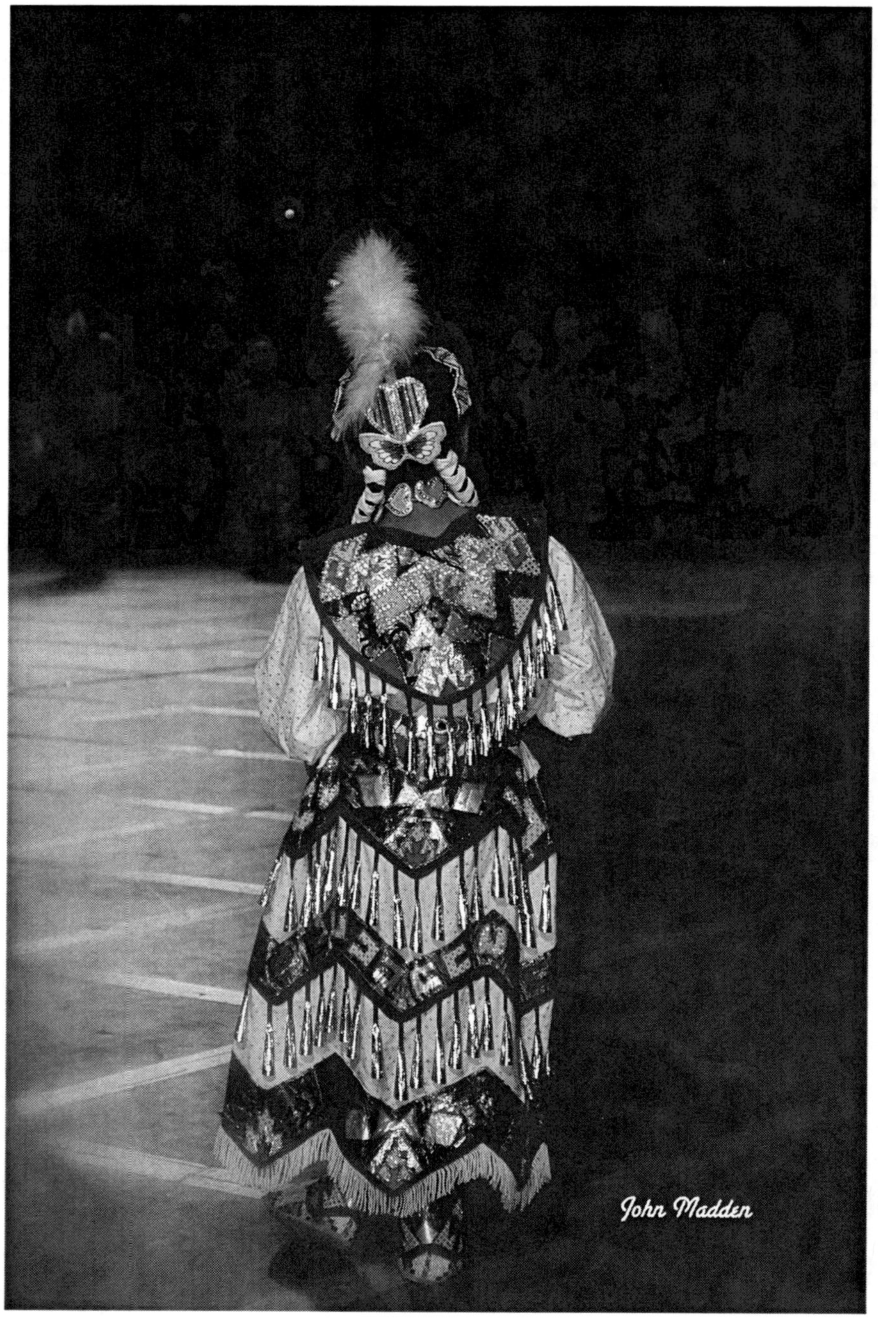
John Madden

Jingle Dress Dancer

Many years ago at the Gathering of Nations Pow Wow (www.gatheringofnations.com), in Albuquerque, New Mexico this young dancer reached out as she danced and captured my undivided attention.

Look at the light on her left side, her tilted stance, the dark (negative space) on her right side, the downward angle of her jingles, and the plume on her headdress.

WOW.... it screams all a photo needs to be. Everything directs me to take photo after photo.

The Gathering is the last Thursday – Saturday of April. It's my favorite Pow Wow and is held in the "Pit" where the University of New Mexico Lobos play basketball.

Little Tykes are children of the adult Pow Wow dancers. As long as I've danced and gone to Pow Wows they're my absolute favorite dancers. As early as diapers they're in regalia, dancing, starting and stopping on the right beat of the drum, and at the same time looking for Mom and Dad.

Sometimes they're dancing with a pacifier and maybe a bottle but they're dancing and holding the beat. At times their diapers are bigger than their regalia, but they dance!

The Jingle dress originated in northern Minnesota from the Pan-Indian community of the Ojibwe. Story goes an elder medicine man had a granddaughter who was very ill. He had a dream and a spirit came to him, wearing a jingle dress, and told him to make one for his granddaughter, to teach her to dance, and she'd get well.

He and his wife made one. Several ladies took her into the circle, danced her around three times and she was healed.

A Jingle dress is made of leather, cloth, or velvet and is covered with jingles made from shiny metal. Now a days lids from snuff cans are bent and rolled into a triangle bell shape, attached to the dress with ribbon or fabric in a design of choice by the dancer.

The pattern is designed to allow the jingles to make them jingle making "happy" sound. The dance is controlled as there are no high kicking or twirls and in a zigzag pattern.

She raises her fan when the "honor beats" are played on the drum. They must stay in beat with the drum and stop both feet on the ground at the end of the song.

. . .

Footnote: Honor beats: honor beats placed at a specific time during the song. The style of honor beats varies some, but is usually four loud beats representing cannon fire in battle; another interpretation: *Honor Beats: strong, heavy beating of the drum—like hearts beating for a common purpose of honoring life, the dance, meaning of the dance, importance of the dance, beating of the heart for life.*

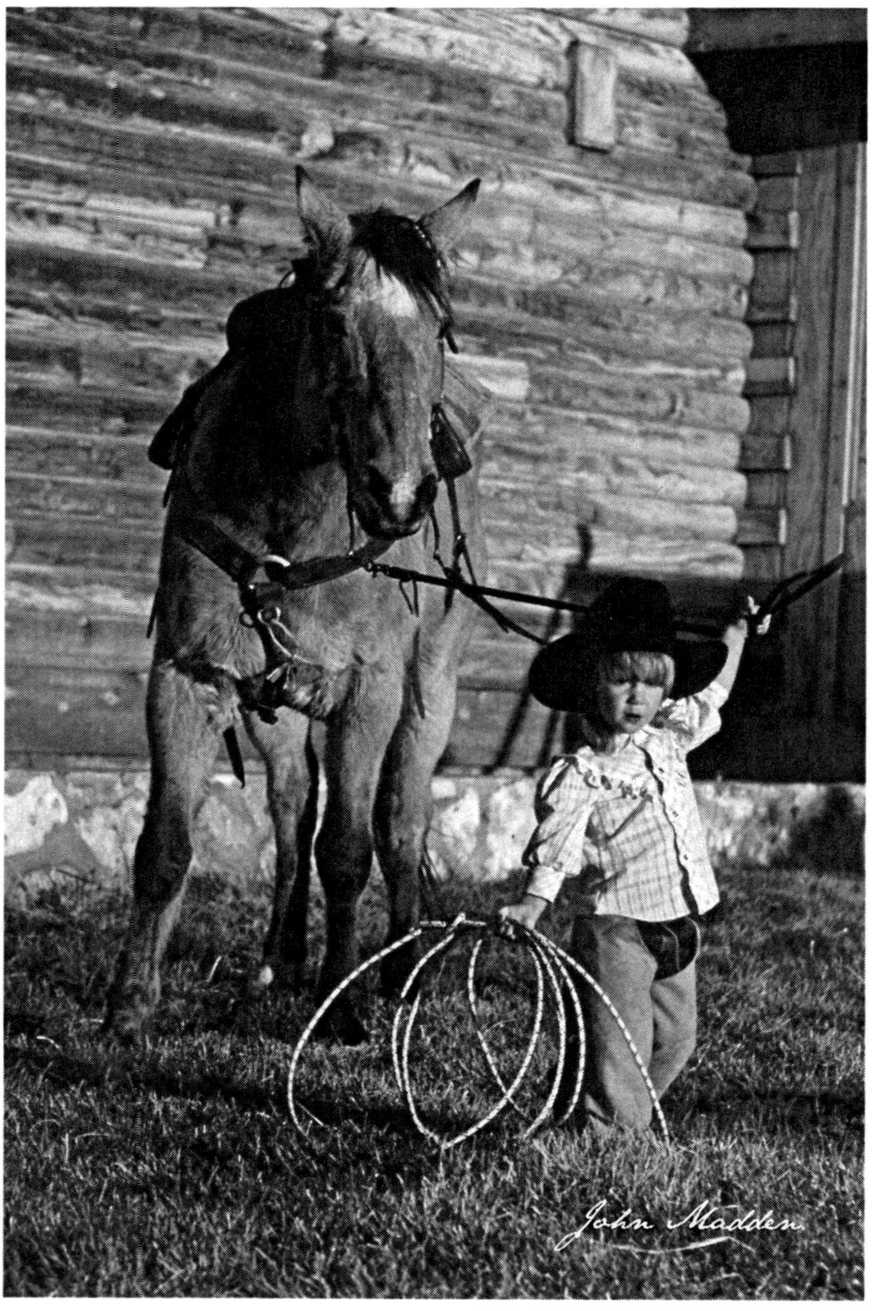
John Madden

Now that's a cowgirl.

A lady friend I worked with told me about her cowgirl daughter and granddaughter, living in New Mexico, The land of enchantment. The more I heard about the daughter the more I wanted to try and photograph her.

Cowgirls are a tough lot of "I can do it myself" and anything a man can do so can I, if not better. My experience is that the majority is also very beautiful. In addition to their looks their strong and positive attitude also makes them attention getters.

They work hard, ride hard, are more than spouses/wives, they're partners on the ranch. Working right along day and night 24/7/360 as the saying goes. You'll find them side by side with their spouse, riding, roping, branding, and working cattle and all the livestock. All while being a wife, raising children, making and managing meals, maintaining the household, getting children to school, many times holding down a job or part- time job in town.

I've seen many a "wannabe" cowgirl in their store bought and color balanced designer never worked in clothes wearing lots of bling and no horse. They're all show and no go. They take a good photo, but look at their hands, in their eyes, and see what's not there.

A real cowgirl!

Sure enough the daughter fit the real, everyday, get- err- done, what's next, I can do it cowgirl, from her cowboy hat to her scuffed up and well worn cowboy boots. The leather straps on her spurs were as rugged as her chaps. They were stained with blood from dehorning cattle, personal cuts, broken bones, grease from working on equipment, water from fixing a water pump, being run over by cattle all of which announced she was all cowgirl and proud of it.

Having worked as a cowboy, in a feedlot, on weekends while in college, I knew and admired real cowboys and cowgirls. This daughter was all "Cowgirl." My goal was to spend as much time with her, as she'd let me, photograph her walking, talking, riding, sitting outside plus time in her house.

Everywhere we went a dog and her daughter, my friend's granddaughter followed us. She was cute, full of life, questions, running, and at the same time never more than a couple feet from her mother.

I took as many photos as fast as I could hit the trigger on my camera. This was an opportunity I wasn't going to get very often, if ever again. Now I'm good at what I do, as a photographer- because I LOVE IT. However talking a total stranger into allowing me to waste her day and routine with questions was above my comfort level. I don't have the BS skills a politician has of getting people to open him or herself up.

Time was not my friend because I only had today.

A noise, behind me, distracted me so I turned around to confront it.

Walking towards me, with her horse, a lasso, and beautiful innocence was the granddaughter. As if manipulated by an unknown photographic force, my camera came up, the trigger started clicking, I was backing up, crouching lower to get on her level and the photo of a real cowgirl exploded into my film.

I guess you could say I had no choice in taking this photo. Planning doesn't always happen the way you want, thank goodness.

"Trust Everyone, but Always Saddle Your Own Horse"
- Unknown

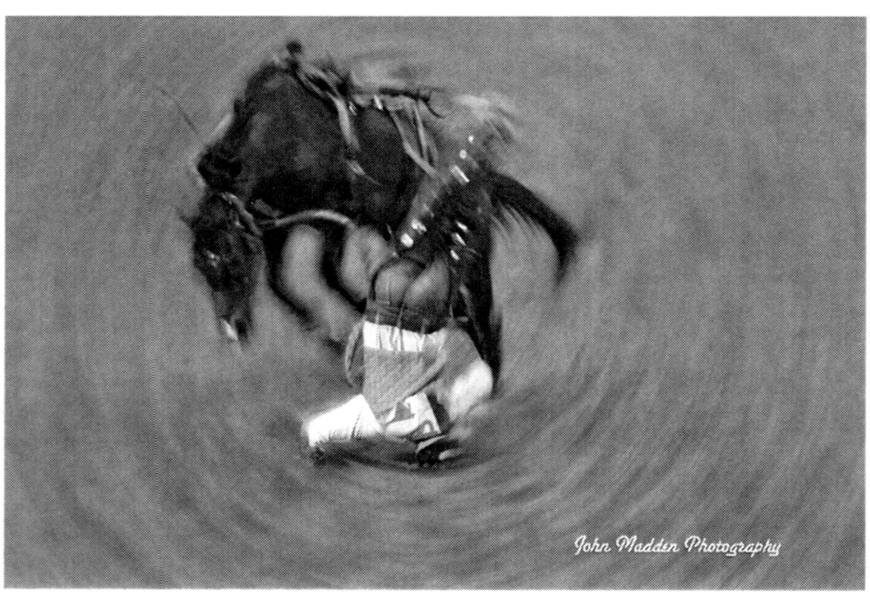
John Madden Photography

Heads UP

The real rodeo is a "Ranch Rodeo." The performers are real, actual, and everyday, hard working ranchers. This is what we do for a living on a ranch, cowboys and cowgirls. They're not Professional Cowboys and Cowgirls from the Professional Rodeo Cowboys Association (PRCA), they're Real Cowboys and Cowgirls doing what they really do, every day.

The Working Ranch Cowboy Association (http://wrca.org) put on the rodeos and 2014 will the 19th year. The office is in Amarillo, Texas. November 6- 9, 2014 they'll have their Championship Ranch Rodeo.

They have 3 objectives other than some of the greatest entertainment you'll see:

- WRCA Mission Statement: To promote ranching on a National and International level and to preserve the lifestyle of the working ranch cowboy.
- WRCA Scholarship Fund: It shall be the mission of the Working Ranch Cowboys Foundation Scholarship Fund to provide financial assistance to working ranch cowboys and their family members showing interest and promise in continuing their education in a collegiate, trade or vocational program.
- WRCA Crisis Fund: It shall be the mission of the Working Ranch Cowboys Foundation Crisis Assistance Fund to provide financial and other assistance to working ranch cowboys and their families who are suffering significant hardships and who are not otherwise able to provide for their needs.

They have events that the day- to- day working cowboys make up of teams from working ranches: grand entry by state and teams, wild cow milking, team branding (they only use a white chalk), ranch bronc riding (this is the wildest and most entertaining event, in my opinion), ranch team sorting (sorting a certain cow from the herd and getting it in a pen), and team doctoring.

A WRCA rodeo is a photographers Christmas! You enjoy action, strength, determination, skill, earned attitude, trying to catch the fast paced action, and stepping out of your comfort zone.

Welcome to my WOW moment- - Heads Up and after landing on his head the rider got up, waved his hat (saying he was okay) and walked off.

"Courage is being scared to death…and saddling up anyway."
- John Wayne

CHAPTER 3

Wildlife

As our civilization grows, expands, grows into the homes and lands of our wildlife they are pushed closer and closer to non- existence.

The following photos and stories represent five of the most powerful, important, beautiful, and honored, especially by Native Americans, samples of God's creation.

The bears and bull buffalo were photographed in South Dakota while the eagle and mountain lion photographed in Texas. All were in protective compounds to some degree which is a shame; but at the same time facing the often unconcerned advance of mankind a growing necessity.

Because of the bears playful nature, at the time, I gave them carton characters names, you'll read how Wayo got his name in his story, the bull buffalo has no name, just it's identity, while the American Eagle is what it is and for the time it's enough.

Look around, Mother Nature's creatures are everywhere, you just have to look and always, always have **FUN**!

"If we can teach people about wildlife, they will be touched. Share my wildlife with me. Because humans want to save things that they love."

- Steve Irwin

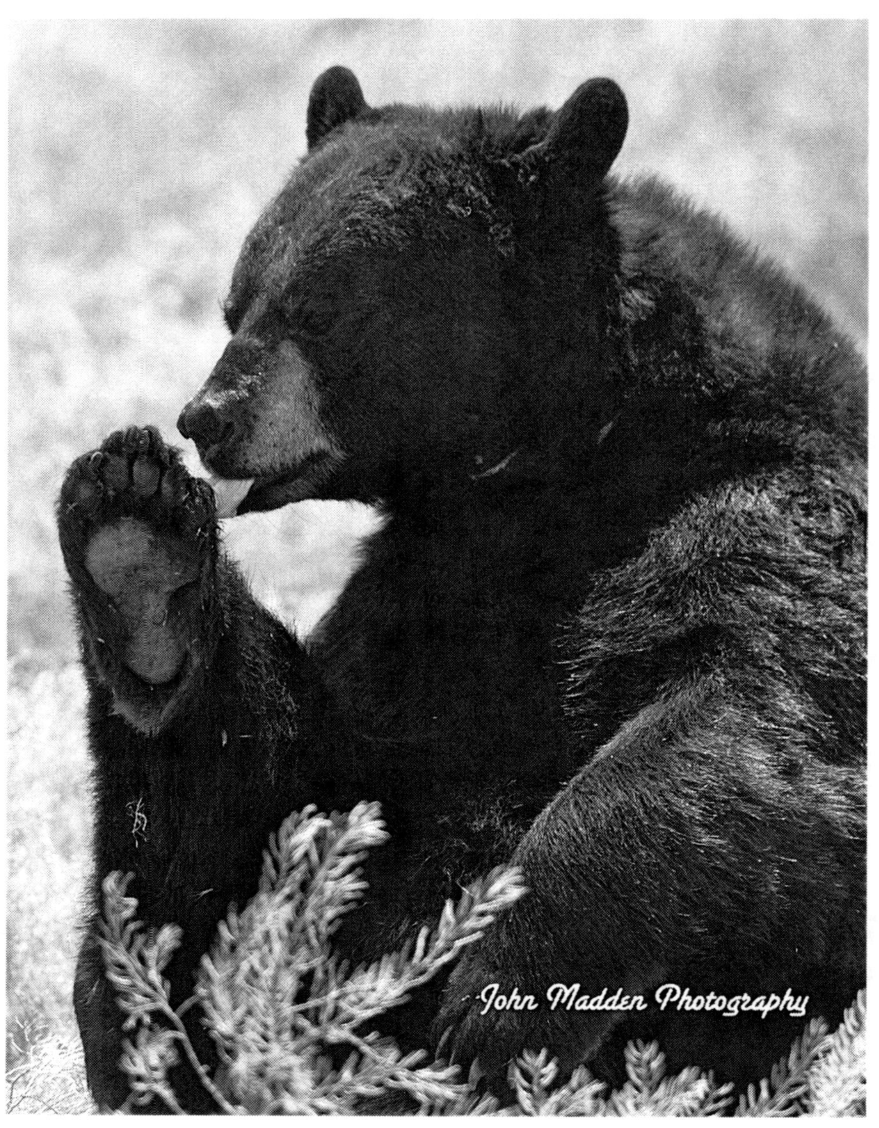
John Madden Photography

Yogi

At Bear Country in South Dakota this BIG one was taking care of basic needs. Licking the Paw!

The wonderful thing about animals is they have as many characteristics as humans. Taking baths, cleaning themselves, finding and eating food, living life as it's presented to them, having babies, raising a family, parents, brothers, sisters, dealing with the environment, and dying.

Think about someone or something coming in and taking the land you've lived your whole life on and you have to adjust. That fits Native Americans and animals to name just a few. Of course they're many other animals and people around the world who fit into this.

In a pasture, taking in the rays, this bear reminded me of "Yogi Bear" and all his actions. Only thing missing was "Boo Boo" playing the straight man (bear as it is) to something Yogi says while licking his paw.

It was a great day to be young at heart and take photo after photo of bears.

Especially "Yogi."

Footnote: The names given Yogi Bear and Boo Boo were/are cartoon characters

"It is never ridicule, but a compliment, that knocks a philosopher off his feet. He is already positioned for every possible counter- attack, counter- argument, and retort... only to find a BIG BEAR HUG coming his way."

- Criss Jami

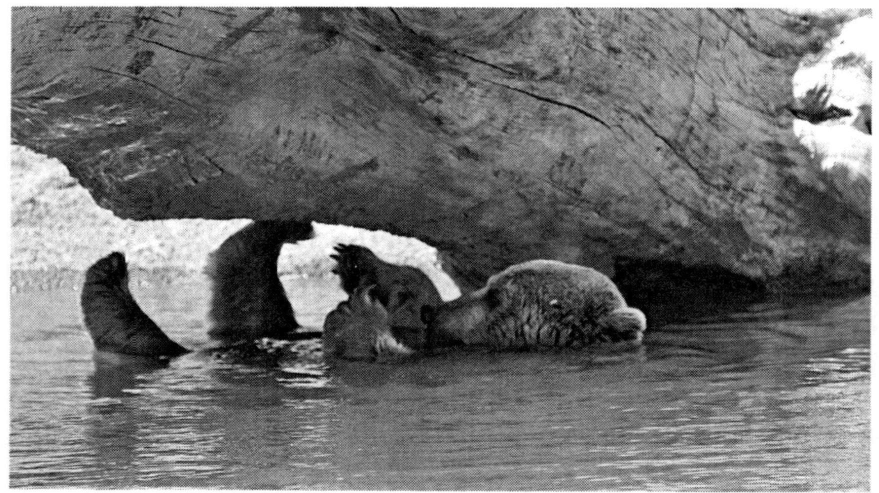

Boo Boo

In South Dakota there's a place called Bear Country at 13820 US 16 outside Rapid City. Besides bear they have nineteen varieties of animals.

Of course they're all fenced in 250 acres. The animals can be observed while you are driving through the park or walking in certain protected areas.

Even though they're fenced in they're not always fenced out and away from you, so a tad of common sense is required. Speaking from personal experience don't think or believe you're 10 feet tall and bulletproof.

They're still animals and you're still human which puts you in their food chain. Oh yes, there are employees all over the place and they're there to help and protect you. You'd be surprised at how some people push the envelope too far, me. After all these photographic years, I'm still surprised at what people will do when they shouldn't. Me.

No preaching or soap boxing, here, just saying the obvious. "Pay Attention To Your Surroundings", it's their home and you're a visitor.

. . .

Bears. Wolves, and buffalo are my trio. Finding them, reading signs, tracking, and photographing them are always on my bucket list.

In a part of the park there's a small pond and in that pond was this bear, taking a bath. How many times do you get to see that? Zero to none.

As I mentioned above pay attention to what's going on around you and what you're photographing. Getting out of the pickup, walking closer to the pond, focusing my camera the presence of large brown and black things around me came to my conscious.

The local community of brown and grizzly bears where ambling my way. Bears can be curious especially in an area where they are looking from the inside, their home, out, where these humans' visitors were.

Again survival instinct trumped more picture taking and the security of a pickup and moving along made the day a great photographic day. WOW happened, thank goodness.

Actually I think this is "Boo Boo" and you'll saw Yogi licking his paw earlier.

> "When you are where wild bears live you learn to pay attention to the rhythm of the land and yourself. Bears not only make the habitat rich, they enrich us just by being."
>
> - Linda Jo Hunter, *Lonesome for Bears: A Woman's Journey in the Tracks of the Wilderness*

CHAPTER 4

Did You Know?

The teddy bear is named after U.S. President Theodore "Teddy" Roosevelt.

In 1902, President Roosevelt participated in a bear- hunting trip in Mississippi. While hunting, Roosevelt declared the behavior of the other hunters "unsportsmanlike" after he refused to kill a bear cub they had captured.

As news of the hunting trip spread, many newspapers around the country featured political cartoons starring "Teddy" and "the bear."

Meanwhile, in Brooklyn, New York, a shop owner named Morris Michtom saw one of the cartoons and had an idea. Michtom and his wife created plush, stuffed bears and placed them in the front window of their shop.

With permission from Roosevelt, Michtom named the bears "Teddy bears." They were an instant success. Ladies and children carried the bears with them in public. President Roosevelt even used the teddy bear as his mascot when he ran for re- election

See more at: http://wonderopolis.org/wonder/how- did- the- teddy- bear- get- its- name/#sthash.ei7ErE2s.dpuf

I want you to be concerned about your next- door neighbor. Do you know your next- door neighbor?

- Mother Teresa

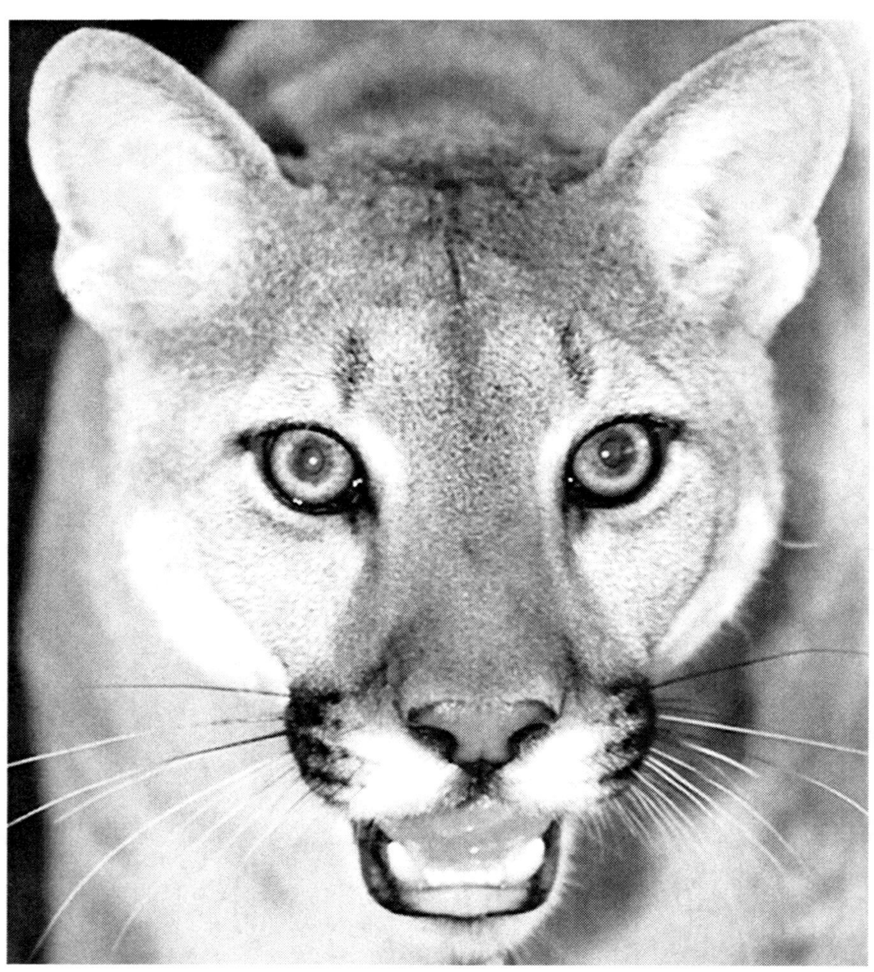

Wayo

A friend of mine, a lady, had a mountain lion, yes a real live, mountain lion: also know as a cougar, panther, mountain cat, cat-amount, or puma.

He lived in a 60′ x 60′ x 25′ tall cage because he couldn't be let out into the wild. Why? Because he was found at 5 months old, in a deserted barn, by a man who already owned a cougar. Wayo and his brother had been abandoned and their front claws had been cut off at the second knuckle on their front paws. This made it impossible for them to be returned to the wild.

He got his name from a very dear friend of both of ours, Monroe Tahmahkera. He's a full blood Comanche and the great grandson of Quanah Parker. She had asked him to give her baby an Indian name.

He studied the mountain lion, watching him play, how he moved, seeing his strength, confidence, and independence even though he wasn't in the wild.

After considerable thought he told her his name was Wayo. She was thrilled her baby had an Indian name and Monroe had given it to him.

She asked him, "What does Wayo mean in Comanche?"

Monroe looked at her and with a strong voice and stern face said "Cat." Comanche's, especially Monroe are pranksters.

Without a smile, but with a smerk he turned and walked away.

Mountain lions live for 8- 13 years in the wild, runs 40- 50 mph,

2′- 3′ in height, 2′- 3′ tail length, adult male averaging 137 lbs, and a adult female averaging 93lbs.

They live in mountains, deserts, rainforests and other diverse places.

An FYI: **Contrary to movies mountain lions produces a variety of vocalizations (sounds), but cannot roar.**

My friend lived in the country, outside Azle, Texas. A friend of hers called and asked her if she'd like a baby mountain lion?

How many people even know someone who has access to or owns a mountain lion, much less owns two, knows someone (a lady) who might want one, and calls the lady to ask her: You want a baby mountain lion?

I know people who have dogs, cats, horses, sheep, goats, and other animals. I've known of folks that give away, sell, trade, or train some of these animals. Known folks who live in the country and have a fair amount of acreage.

But none that fit in any of the above that has and or might call to give away a mountain lion. How about you?

Then let me introduce you to Judy. All 5′2 ½″ and weighting in about 100 lbs. A tad over matching up against a mountain lion, don't you agree?

Another FYI: **His favorite toys are a bowling ball, which he rolls down the slope of his home, picks it up, and hops on his hind legs, carrying the bowling ball back up the slope, drops it on a wood enclosure so it'll roll back down the slope and repeats this over and over again.**

He also likes an empty milk carton that he can squeeze, toss around, and pounce on.

So here I am at her place, her mountain lion is outside it's 25′ tall, 60′ by 60′ encaged metal fence like product on all four sides and on top home.

Oh yea, before I forget this FYI: **They're "extremely fast' in reaching out with a paw, wrapping it around what ever, and pulling it to them. Unbelievably fast! Take my word for it.**

Okay, he's out of his cage with a huge log chain and collar attached to him. So he can't go to far or where she doesn't want him to go.

I'm taking photo after photo of the beautiful animal. He's playing hide- n- seek with me from behind a tree. This is so cool.

As I zoom in closer for a better face shoot I notice my zoom has really reached out and got the photo I want.

I'm getting a great close up, full face, and green eyes, head bouncing up a little.

Head bouncing up and huge log chain following him, not retaining him! For a moment it takes my mind to totally alert my brain, and activate my mouth.... "Judy he's loose and coming my way"

Very lady like she says, "He won't hurt you,"

To which I respond in a highly concerned yet not quite "I'm going to die" voice, "He may not know that!"

She moves between us, grabs his getting smaller, by each step, huge chain, talks to him, he listens, follows her back to his tree, and is secured once again.

She smiles, asks me if I'm okay and I try to hear what I'm saying, but nothing is coming out of my mouth, no voice, only heavy breathing, as I fall backwards.

"Everything is funny, as long as it's happening to somebody else."

- Will Rogers

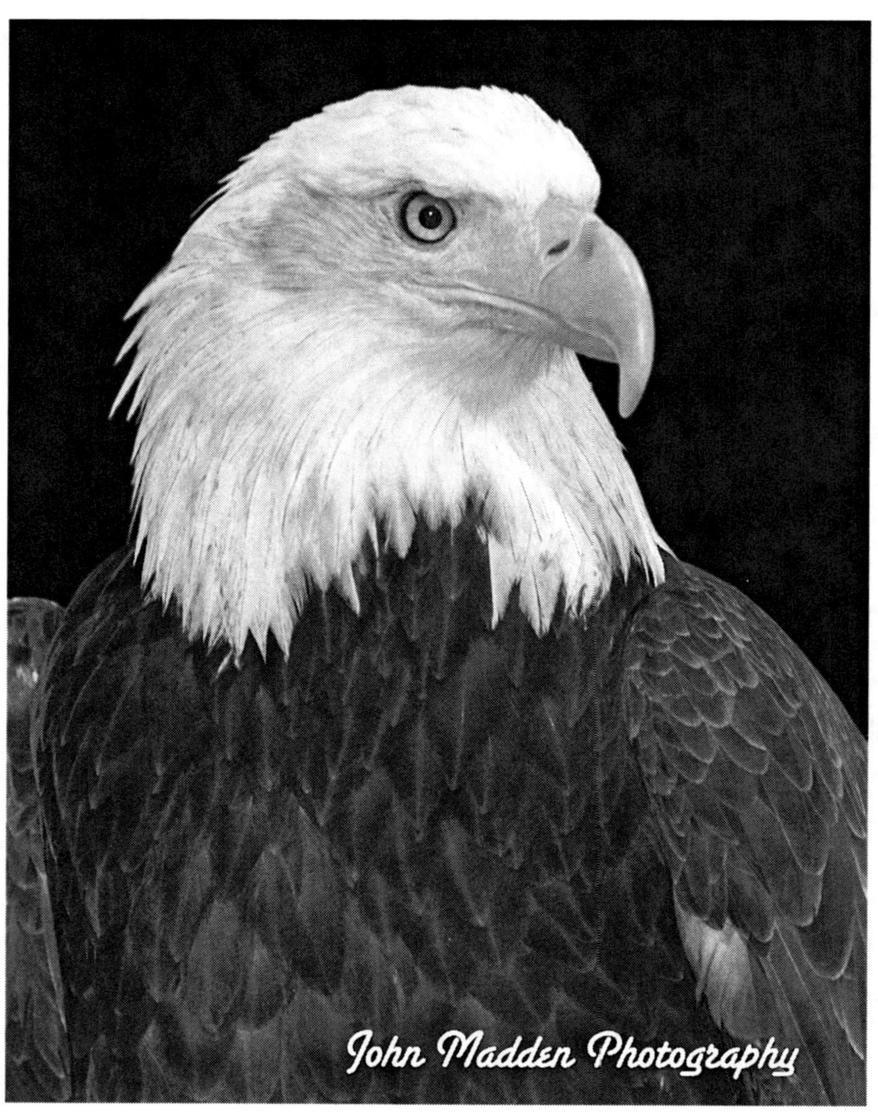
John Madden Photography

American Eagle

A long time friend, Kin Quitugua is the CEO/Executive Director of Hawk Quest from Parker, Colorado. He's a Master Falconer with many years of training, handling, and flies birds of prey, from the Bald (American) and Golden Eagle to the Saw- whet owl. He founded Hawk Quest in 1986. He believes that environmental awareness is critical in saving the world, as we know it, especially for our youth.

Not only that, but he's a heck of nice guy. He takes his program to art shows, schools, scouts, at- risk communities, and anywhere he can show and educate people about our national treasures.

I was fortunate as he allowed me time and the opportunity to photograph this magnificent Bald Eagle. How proud, strong, confident, and independent it is. Truthfully, it was very hard to narrow my choice down to this photo. A book of all the photos I took wouldn't do enough justice to this Bald Eagle.

The Bald Eagle isn't really bald but gets its name from an older meaning of "white headed." The adult is mainly brown with a white head and tail. It's also not only the national bird but also the national animal of the United States of America.

Female Bald Eagles are generally 25% larger than males and female golden eagles are 37% heavier than males.

Many Native American tribes honor the Eagle, both the Bald and Golden. Some tribes call the Golden Eagle the true Eagle.

Eagle Feather Law: Under the current language of the eagle feather law, individuals of certifiable American Indian ancestry enrolled in a federally recognized tribe are legally authorized to obtain eagle feathers. Unauthorized persons found with an eagle or its parts in their possession can be fined up to $25,000. The Eagle Feather Law allows for individuals who are adopted members of federally recognized tribes to obtain eagle feathers and eagle feather permits.

In many societies the Eagle carries prayers to the creator, it flies higher, can see further, is stronger, a sign of good luck and or fortune, represents great power, stability, balance, grace, higher truth, a symbol of a holy spirit, faith, vision, a state of grace, inner peace, and teaches to look beyond and past time and to soar above shadows of life's events.

In movies, many times they'll show an Eagle flying and or circling above for drama. It's very Hollywood and the Eagle always calls down to those below.

FYI: That's like the Western movies when the Indians show up for a fight and the music gets louder and louder. The drums beat, horns blast, all the musical instruments explode in magnificent music. I've talked to many elders and their ancestors have confirmed that music, that orchestra, never showed up in real life.

I can only testified about the Indians, as I haven't had the opportunity to talk to the elders, who talked to their ancestors from the Calvary.

Might have happened for them. Just thinking, if it showed up for Calvary, wonder what happen at the Little Big Horn?

Just wondering.

'Among my activities was membership in the Boy Scouts; I rose each year through the ranks, eventually achieving the rank of Eagle Scout and undertaking leadership roles in organization.'

- Frederick Reines

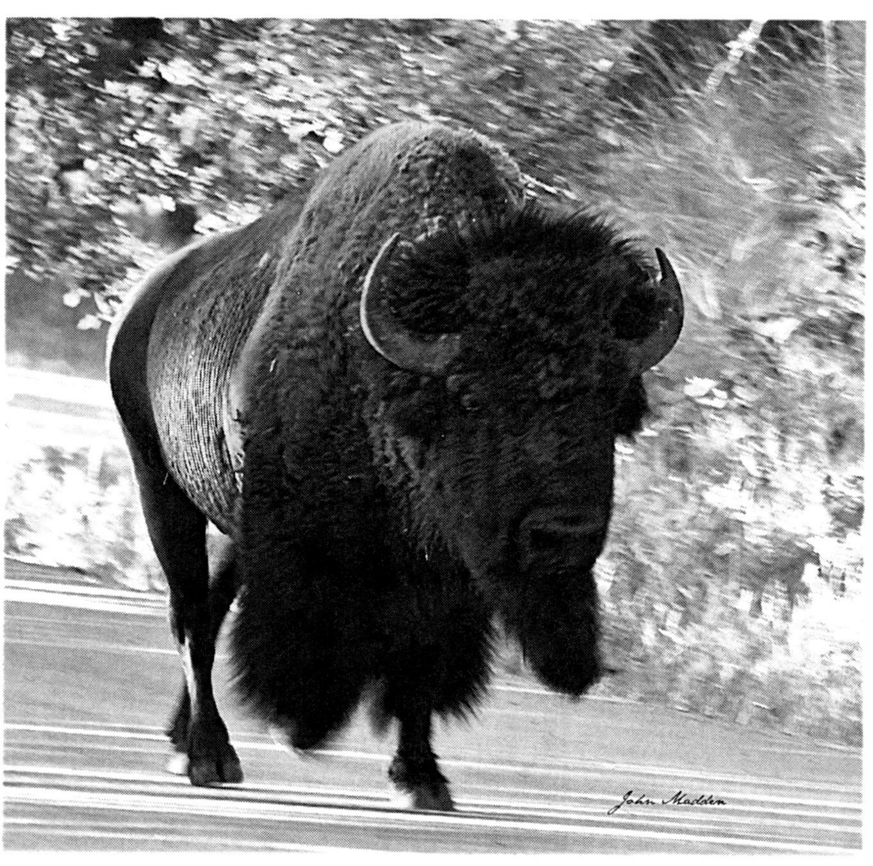
John Madden

Get in the Pickup!

Driving through a park in South Dakota, looking for the buffalo herd, I was running out of road, time and possibilities of seeing any buffalo.

Yea, there's a sign saying something about "You're leaving the park" and all I could do was frown, shake my head and decide what next.

What next came around a curve, a fair size herd of buffalo, babies, mommas and bulls. Hallelujah! That six hour drive wasn't for nothing, there they were and coming right towards me.

I jumped out of my pickup, camera up (this was BD-before digital) so I was shooting blind, so to speak. As fast as I could take a picture I went through a several rolls of 36. They were turning off the road and going up a hill beside it. Standing my ground and rotating I changed film, trying to get as many photos as possible.

As they went up the hill and formed a line going past all I could think of was "shoot, shoot, and shoot more." The herd was bigger than at first sight and it kept coming. Out of the corner of my eye I kind' a caught a vision of a few buffalo coming down the road, bypassing the trek up the hill.

No problem, I turned to photograph them about the time I heard "Get in the Pickup" being screamed at me. It didn't really soak in, as I was too busy. Snap, snap my camera as I again heard "Get in the Pickup!" It was much louder and more emotional.

What? Is how I felt and can't you see I'm busy! I've got to get as many photos as I can, this may never happen again.

The 3rd, 4th or 5th "Get in the Pickup" finally got my attention and I turned to confront this disturbance. As I turned my head from straight in front to my right, I noticed a BIG BROWN BLUR.

Somehow my photography ego reached up and slapped my face hard enough for me to realize that BIG BROWN BLUR was a even BIGGER BULL BUFFALO coming right at me, my pickup door, with nothing between him and me other than that door, with the window DOWN.

As if being pulled in by some unseen force I was in my pickup, door was shut; window was open as his horns passed in review, so to speak. They would have been in the window frame had the door not been shut.

One sneeze, one turn left, a curious hesitation and look left and his horns and most of his head would have been in the driver's seat. Which is where I was. As he passed his head was above the top of my pickup. His back was about a foot taller than the truck. Truthfully I'm fairy confident his back was 10"- 12" above my pickup and a full grown bull can weigh up to 2,000 pounds. Thankfully he wasn't interested in teaching me anything above "BIG BUFFALO BULL trumps 6'3" man and his pickup truck.

To this day I can hear him snort as he passed by. Thankfully God still had things for me to do.

This photo with a different WOW meaning is the result.

WOW that was close!

> "Even if you're on the right track, you'll get run over if you just sit there."
>
> - Will Rogers

CHAPTER 5

Landscapes

Growing up as an AFB (Air Force Brat) and being in Boy Scouts is like growing up all over the world. This includes living in eight states, visiting and traveling through 20 more, 15 foreign counties including Switzerland and especially Germany resulting in landscapes having a special place in my heart. To my total disappointment, I wasn't into photography when I was in Switzerland. Can you believe that? To my defense I was only 11 or 12 at the time.

When I'm traveling, mostly driving, I constantly wonder; what people settled and lived here? What did they do for a living? What was it like? Why did they leave? What was it like to travel in a covered wagon, heading west and suddenly you're under attack? What stories could the landscapes tell if they could talk?

It was hard to narrow down so many landscape photos to the two enclosed. Truth being, the more experience I have, and the better my landscapes have become. I was at a photography gathering once where you could have heavy- duty professionals critique your work.

As I've said, I've never had a photography lesson, but have been to three Dewitt Jones (http://www.dewittjones.com/) photography seminars. He doesn't critique he encourages.

Okay, back to the heavy- duty professional critiquing of my work. She told me to stick with a different subject matter.

That positive input cost me $50.00. It was good of her to be so straight forward, but I didn't pay much attention as prior to that and definitely afterwards landscapes were and have been my second best sellers. With the exception of "Resurrection" which I've included in the Spiritual section. It's by and far the best seller I've been blessed to capture.

More important than being my best seller it has been and continues to be the one that impacts people more, has been viewed in more countries, and has actually made people cry. It's the gift that keeps on giving over and over to so many.

Both these photos have a deep meaning to me, I'm happy to share them with you, and hope you enjoy them. Point being do what you love, enjoy every experience, have faith in yourself, believe in what you're doing, trust your instincts, and above all have fun.

"Dance is the **landscape** of a man's soul"

- Unknown

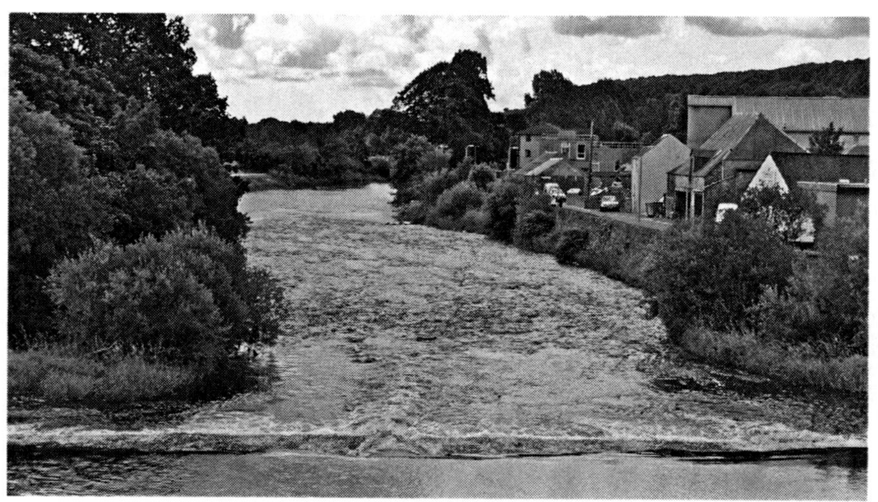

Scotland River

Why indeed take this photo? I have no idea of it's name, the name of the town in Scotland, or anything about it.

Have you ever seen something or someone and wondered: what's the history, how did it get it's name, did it play an important part of or in someone's life, where did it come from, how did it get created, or just get lost in it?

As mentioned in other stories, in the summer of 2009 I was fortunate to go the Ireland, Northern Ireland, Scotland, England, and Paris with the Kwahadi Dancers.

We crossed this river and spent some time in its town. Taking a break from riding we had some time to look around and take in the wonderful atmosphere. There was a small parade going down the only street with floats, happy people, and very welcome for road weary Kwahadi Dancers.

Across the street, there was a small group of women playing tubs, singing and having more fun as every moment passed.

It was an unexpected treat and I probably only took a hundred or so photos. That's kind of a slow photo opportunity for me.

Walking around I went back to the bridge to see if I could get some photos of the river rocks. I love rocks and the challenge of capturing them engulfs my artistic boundaries.

As I looked down and tried to capture the river rocks the river itself drew my attention. Where did it start? How old was it? Where did it go? How strong was the current? Do people raft, intertube it, canoe, or kayak it?

I've done all the above on many rivers in New Mexico and Texas. Oh, what a joy this river would be. Look at it; it just calls to be a part of ones day, week, and life.

Take a moment, look deep into the photo, close your eyes and be there. Feel the current, coldness of the water, be a part of nature, feel the sun on your face, stretch your arms as you dip your paddle into the water, feel the pull on your muscles, feel the water as you glide over it, feeling the ripples of the river under you, move and turn your paddle to the side to make the bend in the river.

Can you see, in your mind, horses carrying their riders across it? Are they soldiers? Are they warriors going or coming from a battle. Maybe a family out for an afternoon rides. Or long lost lovers riding to a rendezvous after a separation? Maybe it's children playing?

Have you ever run a river?

Are the bends sandy, rocks, dirt, cliffs, or what? A river rat wants and needs to know.

"How could drops of water know themselves to be a river?
Yet **the river** flows on"

- Antoine de Saint

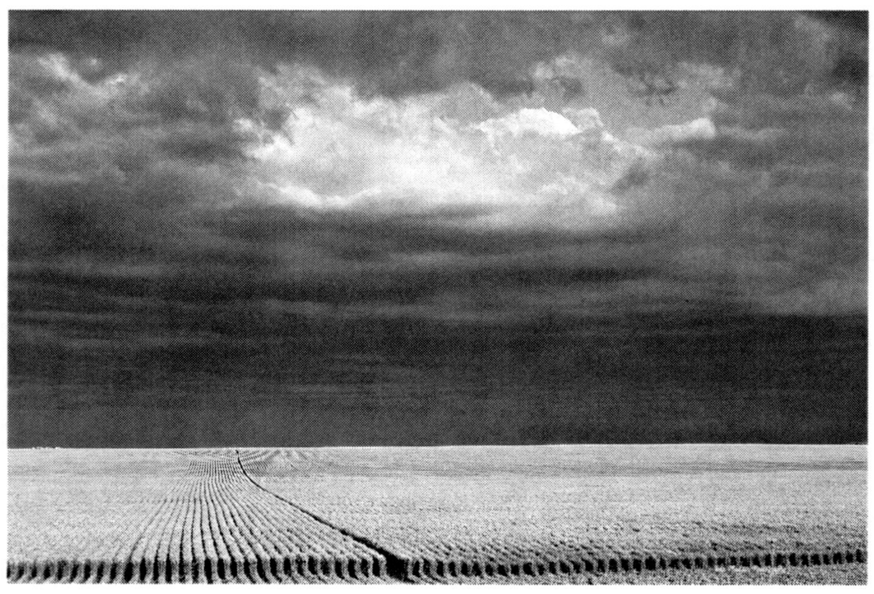

Colorado Wheat Field

Driving to the Pine Ridge Reservation, in South Dakota, through NE Colorado and after rounding a left hand curve, I glanced at the wheat field. Glanced being the optimum word, I noticed a bright yellow field, a cut of some kind through it and I hit my brakes.

Not the thing to do when you're going over seventy mph and pulling the biggest trailer that U- Haul had for rent. But, there was a moment when I thought I saw WOW and had to find out for sure.

Backing up about two miles, on a narrow Colorado one- lane road with traffic behind and in front, well, let's just say. Don't!

Ah, it was a WOW! Traffic was such that I dare not get out of my pickup. There wasn't a shoulder, except for a slight drop off of about a small cliff of about a foot. I could just see pickup and trailer lying on their side.

I got a couple one- finger salutes and comments I couldn't hear, which was best. Still, what a photo this was if only I could get it with all the traffic and anti- support from fellow travelers.

Okay, rolled my window down, got my camera (BD) and started shooting. Watch out dude you almost hit my pickup truck or where you trying to get my camera? On top of the helpful, NOT, traffic the wind decided to join the circus. Of course it was coming straight out of the West. You guessed it, the direction I was trying to shoot.

Part of being a photographer is dealing with, adjusting to, figuring out, and living with Mother Nature.

I did and here it is!

"The Lord said 'let there be wheat' and Saskatchewan was born."

- Stephen Leacock

Sometimes things just don't work out

Everyone has or will have one of those days when things just don't work out, right?

Let me take a few minutes to tell you about **THREE** of mine.

Many years ago at **Raton, New Mexico at the NRA Whittington Center** I was at a "Rendezvous" with Mountain Men, period reenactor soldiers, reenactor settlers, frontiersmen, Native Americans, drum and buglers, present- day folks with their families.

There was black power shooting, axe throwing, bow and arrow shooting, knife throwing, flint napping, arrow making, foods from the period, trade goods for sale including clothes, beads, furniture, jewelry, knives, bow and arrows, shoes, boots, and moccasins, cooking equipment, and a parade with an old historical American Flag.

I got in front of the parade which had a Mountain Man carrying this beautiful flag, a drummer on one side, a flute player on the other, dressed and looking like they had just come from a battle. They had bandages on their heads and different places on their bodies, and as they played and walked mountain men, soldiers, settlers, Native Americans, frontiersmen and women fell in behind them.

Can you see it? It was truly a step back in time, history unfolding before me. What a photographic opportunity and experience.

This was before digital so it was click, click, and more clicks as I backed up. Keeping track mentally, a necessary trick I learned so as not to have to keep looking at the counter on the camera, I hit close to 36, wound the roll, opened the back of my camera, had already pulled another roll out of my pocket to insert into the camera, pulled the used roll out, put in the new roll, and closed the camera back. I put the used roll in my pocket and as was my habit felt my pocket to slide the roll deeper into my pocket.

Wait a minute.

I couldn't feel the used roll of film. I looked on the ground, had I dropped it? Perplexed I looked on the ground, standing still not moving so as to not kick it or step on it. Reaching back into my pocket I emptied it. No film. Okay, I had to have dropped it, starting walking towards the oncoming parade because I had dropped it. No film.

Checking my shirt pockets, I never put my film there, but maybe this time. No film. I checked out my other front jean pocket and the rear pockets. No film.

I stood there as the parade literally passed by me, looking everywhere and not believing the reality of "I didn't have any film in my camera to start with."

NO!

At the **International Balloon Festival Albuquerque, New Mexico** years ago, I had gotten up at 4 AM to go to the area where the balloons would be launched. It was dark as dark could be but if you've ever see hot air balloons light up in the dark, you know what a thrill it is and something you don't want to miss if possible.

As I walked to the grounds I had to walk up a small hill. It was flat on top and there were people sitting on blankets, drinking wine, eating cheese and other snacks with a "Morning" and an offer to share whatever that had. Too early for me I thanked them and went down to the field.

I love photographing the hot air balloons, they're colorful, artistic, comical, serious, and extremely beautiful when they light up and lift off. Everyone is happy, full of life, talking, laughing, usually cold, and it's controlled mass confusion.

Watching the crews work to loft their balloon sometimes is a comedy act all to itself. There always seems to be a "newbie" who is so anxious to help that they're in the way.

The patience of the experienced crew is fun as they try to counter what the newbie has or hasn't done and at the same time encouraging the newbie.

It's truly a team/crew effort and as the balloon lifts higher and higher a cheer goes up to the pilot and passengers. The pilot and passengers thrown down, so to speak, a cheer of appreciation as they enter the silence and grandeur of the journey.

On one occasion, as the balloon lifts, the pilot turned back to the ground crew and yelled "Mamma, what do I do now?" He was grinning from ear to ear, his wife was laughing so hard she couldn't stand still. His ground crew laughed and cheered louder. I didn't see a lot of smiles or hear cheers from his passengers.

About 11 AM I give up and head back to the motel. I'm tired, hungry, thirsty, in need of a potty break, and looking forward to a shower. I take the elevator up 5 floors to my room, slip off my shoes, shed my coat, sweater, hat, and step out on the balcony.

Scanning the sky for balloons I see several with the mountain, Sandia Crest, behind them about the same time as I see the Air Force Thunderbirds fly between the balloons and me. Camera.... get my camera is all I could think. What a photo!

Racing back inside, I look for my camera. Where is it? Okay, where did I put it? I quickly search the room as the truth slowly soaks in my tired brain.

It's 5 floors downstairs, in my locked pickup, in the secured parking garage.

NO!

I'm at the **Battleground of the Little Bighorn** (http://www.nps.gov/libi/historyculture/battle- of- the- little- bighorn.htm) in Montana, where Lt Col. George Custer spent his last day. It's a beautiful National Cemetery, well- manicured, green grass, trees, museum, and a self- tour of the battleground.

On June 25, 1876 saw 268 soldiers of the 7th Calvary and somewhere around 80 Lakota and Cheyenne dead. Fifty two percent of Custer's commands were casualties. Custer, his younger brother Tom Custer (he received 2 Congressional Metal of Honors in his youthful 20 years), another brother, a nephew and a brother- in-law lay dead.

One reason: Historians think a village of around 8,000 Indians of mostly Teton Lakota plus Cheyenne and a small number of Santee Sioux and Arapaho with somewhere between 1,500- 1,800 warriors. Custer's Battalion of 700 men were greatly outnumbered and a little over 370 of those were from foreign countries. Can you imagine the communication problems?

Remember all those beautiful paintings of Custer standing in the middle of all his troopers, fighting the Indians. There was a "small" area where that's partly true as the battlefield is spread out for miles. Graves spread out following a trail of white makers.

As I slowly took in the magnitude of the defeat I noticed a horse and rider in the distance. I took out my 100- 300 lens and could barely make the rider was Native American carrying shield, lance, with a bow and arrows as he rode up and down the outer boundaries of the line of white marble graves. I couldn't get a good shot, so I drove, walked, and ran trying to get close enough for a good photo. It was warm and I didn't have enough water with me. Still I continued to get a good angle so I could get a good photo.

Oh, yea, this too was before digital. I shot several rolls of film, careful to secure them in my jeans pocket. We keep up this running, so to speak, contest, him riding and me trying to get a good photo for over an hour or two.

Finally he's riding in my direction. Come on, come on just one more small hill and I've got you. Even from the distances I could tell he was dressed in regalia, painted for war, singing and chanting as he rode. He would yell, hold up his lance and shield, sometimes commanding his horse to run hard and fast.

Okay, he just dropped behind that hill and when he comes out on top, I got him! He topped the hill, stopped, raised both his lance and shield, looked down towards me, yelled, pulled the reins back and his horse raised up on his hind legs just about the time I heard my camera rewind that used up roll of film! In a moment he was there and the next he was gone!

NO, not again!

All I can do is see these three photos in my memory. Sometimes things just don't work out!

> "A well adjusted person is one who makes the same mistake twice without getting nervous."
>
> - Alexander Hamilton

CHAPTER 6

Spiritual

I realize this title might make some of you blink and wonder, "Why?"

Simple, that's the way I feel about these photos and the stories. I was raised in a church going, greatly referred to as Christian, home but with no judgment concerning other religions and or beliefs. My grandmother Sheppard raised me to believe in God, his love, forgiveness, and to respect all faiths. The greatest part of my church raising was in military Chapels, non- denominational.

Growing up in South Dakota and the Southwest with Native Americans I've experienced many roads of beliefs.

In studying my ancestry many came from the Catholic and Baptist churches while I grew up in non- denominational and Methodist churches.

I believe my diversity, honoring, appreciating and understanding of these different beliefs has given me such a devout love, passion, interest in and for spiritual things, places, beliefs, churches, crosses, and especially Catholic churches. The architect and pageantry of the Catholic churches draw me to them like a bee to honey, especially the Spanish culture that affects the churches of New Mexico.

The Pueblo wars of New Mexico were a direct result of Spanish soldiers and priests who were intent on converting the Pueblo Indians to Christianity and prevented them from following their cultures and traditions from 1680- 1692 dictating that they abandon their tribal religious beliefs.

The Spanish Christian architect is majestically captured in the churches they touched, as a few are included for your pleasure. Also included are three very spiritual moments in my life.

"Music is the mediator between the spiritual and the sensual life."

- Ludwig van Beethoven

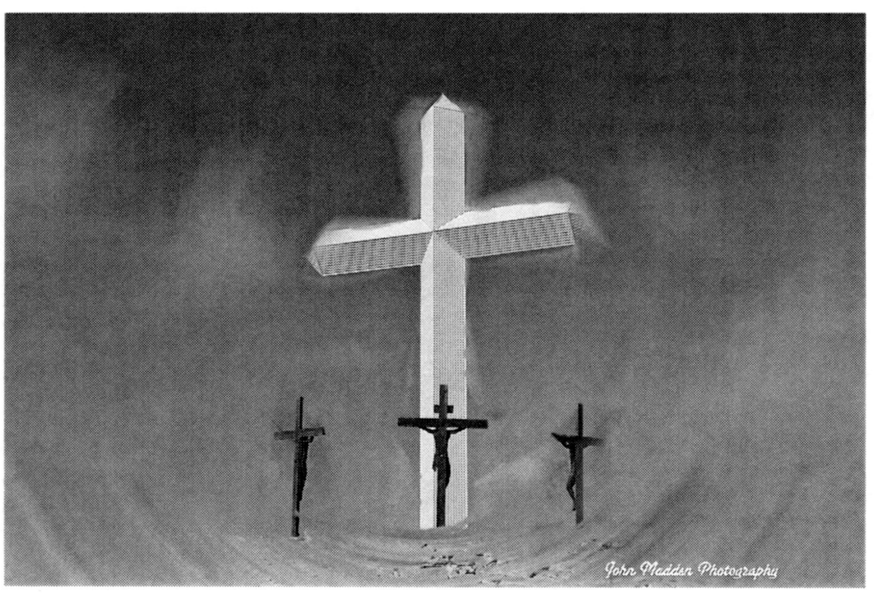
John Madden Photography

The Crosses

Just off I- 40 at Groom, Texas stands the "Cross of our Lord Jesus Christ Ministries" (www.crossministries.net). The cross is nineteen stories high, an 11 story- arm span, , weighs 1,250 tons or 2.5 million pounds, it can be seen from 20 miles away, construction took 8 months and 10 million people pass it every year.

Groom is around 45 miles east of Amarillo, Texas.

Steve Thomas and his wife Bobby built it and it was a family project for the Thomas family. It's open 24/7 with no charge to visit or spend the night. Gifts make this ministry a reality.

Beside the cross there are bronze sculptures of the 12 steps leading to Jesus' crucifixion, fountain of living water, Jesus taken down from the cross, Saint Michael the Archangel, the empty tomb and the Last Supper. Mickey Wells was the sculptor. The sculptures and the three crosses are in this photo.

It's a spiritual experience to be there as the Holy Spirit wraps around you and is with you as you slowly take it all in.

As I progressed from sculpture to sculpture and through the gift shop I keep coming back to the three crosses, on a rise, behind the cross, sculptures, and gift shop. Walking to them I envisioned being at Calvary and seeing the after effect.

I saw it as a blur and when I downloaded the photo of the photo gifts of the day, this is what I saw in my minds eye.

At night, floodlights surround it up for all to see, like a Lighthouse offering safe passage. You have to see it sometime. It's awe- inspiring and gives one the sense of God's love wrapped around them.

"Freedom prospers when religion is vibrant and the rule of law under God is acknowledged."

- Ronald Reagan

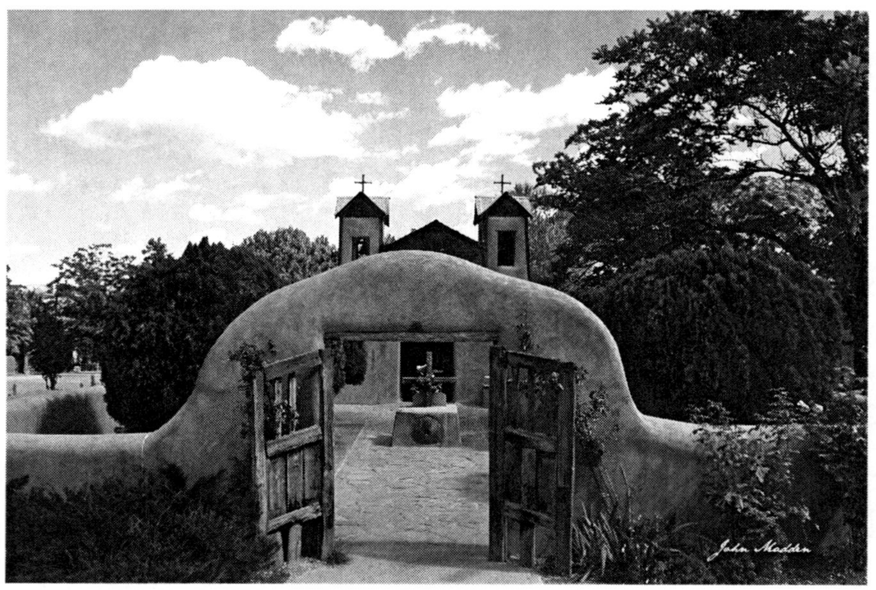
John Madden

El Santuario de Chimayo

Many years ago, a friend told me about this church and took me to it. The moment you step out of the pickup and see it, you're captivated by its presence. It's a magnificent adobe structure surrounded by shops, crosses, another smaller church, and an aura of warmth, healing, sacrament, a walled courtyard, and peace.

In 1805 the site's clay was the source of healing power. Currently a small room called "el pocito" has a round pit in it holding the "holy dirt" (tierra bendita), which is believed to have healing power.

The Church replaces the dirt, as needed, from nearby hillsides up to 25 to 30 tons a year. That's a lot of dirt, holy dirt, going all over the world for healing.

Belief is one of our strongest qualities.

That small room, which most people have to duck to enter, is attached to a larger room with photos, crutches, walkers, canes, wheel chairs, candles, and stories of healings. Both rooms are attached to the sanctuary,

Yearly some 30,000 people from everywhere in the world, make a pilgrimage there during Holy Week, especially on Holy Thursday and Good Friday. Annually approximately 300,000 visit.

Many walk, but I've seen people crawling, walking on their knees, in wheel chairs, on crutches, walkers, in carts pulled by family and or animals, and riding in all sorts of vehicles. Walking with and among them you feel their energy, desire for the pilgrimage, sense of fulfillment, and the satisfaction of making it. Think of if as a "Spiritual Marathon" and close your eyes while you visualize their victory.

Take a moment to nod your head, smile, and celebrate with them.

On the 4th weekend of July the feast of St. James the Great (Santigao) is celebrated.

In 1970 El Santuario de Chimayo was declared a National Historic Landmark. It's been called "the most important Catholic pilgrimage center in the United States."

It's more than a piece of history, a place of healing, a beautiful adobe building, it's a spiritual experience that stays with you and fills you with the love it gives freely.

It's just outside Espanola, NM between Santa Fe and Taos near the high road to Taos.

For me, when I'm in the area, it's a must and I'm a Methodist.

"The camera sees more than the eye, so why not make use of it?"

- *Edward Weston*

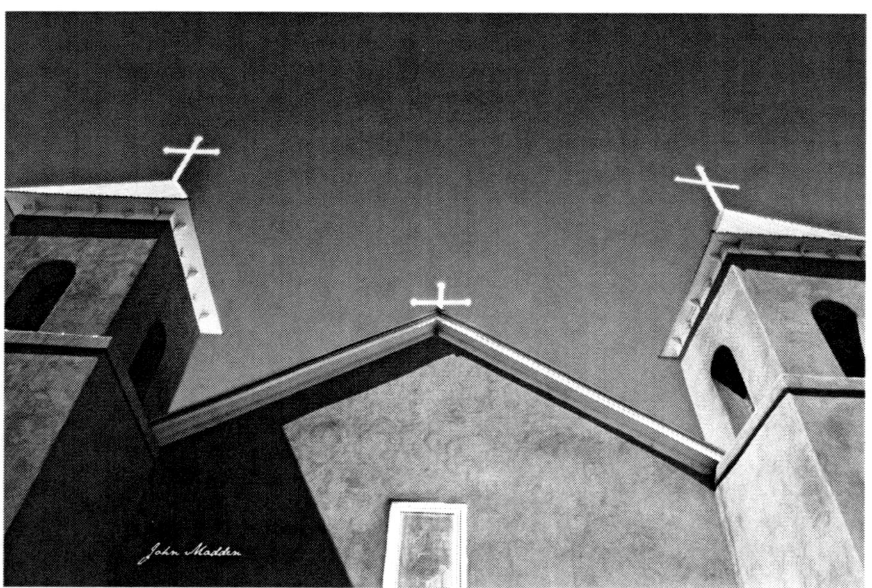
John Madden

Santa Cruz de la Cañada

Church is about twenty- five miles north of Santa Fe, NM and just east of Espanola, NM on state road 76. It was built around 1730 and is the biggest and best mission church in New Mexico.

It belongs to the Diocese of Santa Fe. Sons of the Holy Family Priests and Dominican Sisters serve the Holy Cross School.

Catholic churches, especially in New Mexico, are a favorite photographic experience for me. I love their grandeur as well as their simplicity. It's been my experience that they have fantastic alters, history, architecture, and photographically, they're like unwrapping a Christmas gift 365 days a year.

I've driven by and photographed the church many times getting some "okay" photos. This time the strength of the two towers and 3 crosses were so powerful and compelling that I pulled over, got out of my pickup, grabbed my camera, and walked, as if lead, into the courtyard.

It was as if the towers and crosses were looking down to me not at me and talking to me. There was a power generating from them to my camera and into my being. How could I not submit to their call?

> "And know that I am with you always; yes, to the end of time."
>
> - Jesus Christ

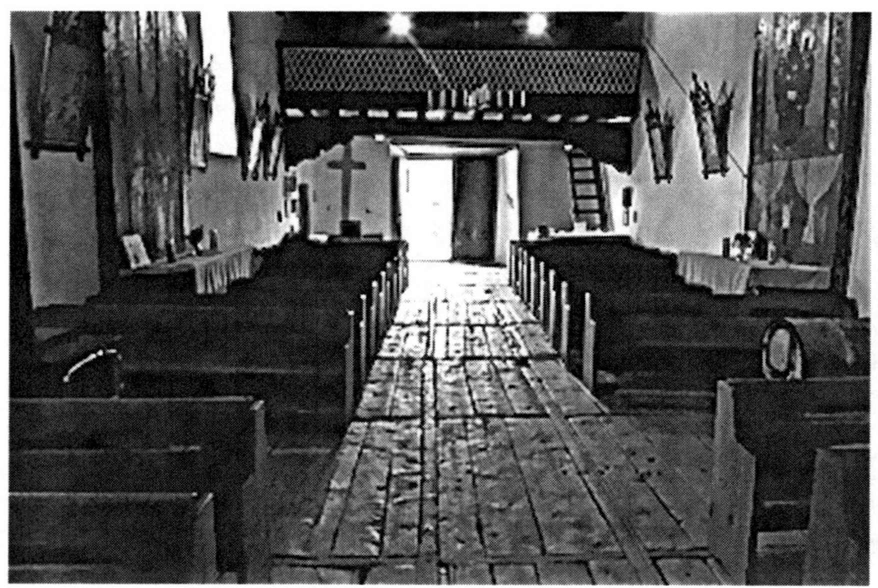

San Jose de Garcia at Las Trampas, NM

March 4, 2002 while on a personal photographic tour of New Mexico, I found this church. It's on NM 76 also called the High Road to Taos. It's between Santa Fe and Taos. NM.

The original name was Santo Tomas del Rio de las Trampas. It was built between 1760- 1776. In 1970 it became a National Historical Landmark.

The church didn't have a priest and services would only happen if and when a visiting priest was available. Hence it was locked up and there wasn't anyone around who knew who had a key to get in.

The outside is adobe plaster. It's guarded by an adobe wall with a high walled entrance. A cemetery rests on one side with those honored to be there. On the other side a small iron fence surrounds a cross of metal and wood, obviously another grave.

It took three years to find the "holder of the Key" and lots of talking to get him to unlock the church. Walking in was truly a walk into the past.

Looking up at the ceiling designs I found out they are from the 18th and 19th century. Walking up the isle was wonderful; the floor was made of wooden timbers. You could see how they planed them to make them flat.

The altar was a carved masterpiece from floor to an overlap onto the ceiling, all wood, all carved, colorful and breathtaking.

The twelve steps of the crucifixion were also carved, painted and hanging around the walls of the church.

Facing the altar then turning to the left was a glass case with five of the most elaborate priest robes. Having been in Catholic churches and services I've seen what priest's wear. I have never seen anything, absolutely nothing as ornate and beautiful as these.

Standing there viewing them and looking around the church questions of who wore these, what were they like, what were the church members like, what history these walls have seen and heard, and what's to become of this beautiful historical church?

"Dream the dream, find that extraordinary vision, and keep it in focus."

- Dewitt Jones

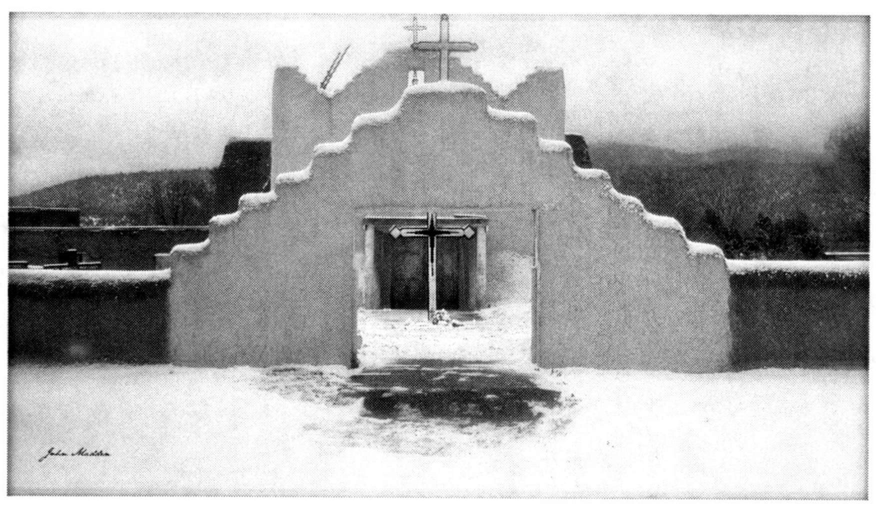

San Lorenzo Church Picruis Pueblo

December 19, 2013 we were setting up for a FREE Give- Away of clothes, toys, household goods, books, shoes, boots, coats, costume jewelry, games, and many other items to the Native Americans living at pueblos and on reservations. Helping others, especially Native Americans, is our mission.

In seven years we've helped over 6,500 people in over 50 tribes. Native Americans, our ancestry, have the highest number of diabetics, highest number of alcoholics, suicides, and unemployment rates. Historically every treaty, signed by the US has been broken. That experience naturally created a lack of trust for outsiders.

Our decision came about due to Monroe Tahmahkera, he was our dear friend and great grandson of Quanah Parker, both Comanche. Monroe was a pied piper of people and was the most loving, giving, sharing, and low- key person. To know him was a blessing.

He taught giving to those in need. In honor of him we created 4DirectionsInc. (www.facebook/fourdirectionsinc) and (http://fourdirections- helping- hands.blogspot)

Have you ever been drawn to something, as if it has an unknown deity who was pulling, pushing, directing, and encourages you to something?

As we drove up the Picruis Pueblo where they have 80%- 90% unemployment, their church stood directly behind the administration office. Having been there before I've photographed it inside and outside. It was one of those churches that didn't stay in your memory as unique or memorable.

As we unloaded all the things we'd brought, it started snowing, with those big heavy flakes that cover everything. The snow made a small lake and the hills behind it grab my attention. It has snowed on us all the way from Amarillo to Picruis and snow was calling me to come out and play in it with my camera.

Not being one that's good at waiting, after several hours, but probably 10 minutes max, of torture, I gave in and went to capture the snow, lake, and hill. Click, click and while nice I was empty.

This photographer can't be photographly empty and happy at the same time.

Turning around to go back to the old museum, where we were putting everything, WOW I saw the church. Snowflakes, those BIG ones, were gracefully falling, on the church, fence, crosses, and mountain behind the church.

Question: Can Mother Nature do something like that to capture ones attention?

Answer: Yes, every day. Right Dewitt!

It was beyond beautiful and it totally wrapped itself around me and in my heart. Everything jumped out at me as if posing for a National Geographic or some famous photographer to record the moment for all eternity. It was just like Ansel Adams did for the Moon over Hernandez on November 1, 1941.

Instead it had me and I was so thrilled I was afraid it would stop snowing and melt before I could take a few fast photos.

To me, and I'll admit I'm very opinionated, it's one of the best photos I've ever been blessed to stumble into and record for all time.

"The children were lined up in the cafeteria of a Catholic elementary school for lunch. At the head of the table was a large pile of apples. The nun made a note, and posted on the apple tray: 'Take only ONE . God is watching.' Moving further along the lunch line, at the other end of the table was a large pile of chocolate chip cookies. A child had written a note, 'Take all you want. God is watching the apples."

- Unknown

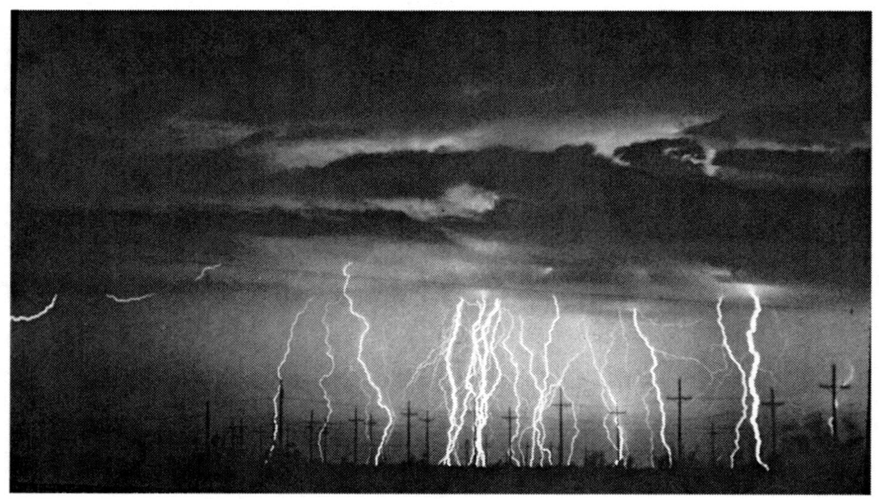

Resurrection

For years I've loved rain, thunder, and lightning. I had heard the old stories of:

Thunder is God bowling.

When it rains, thunders, and there is lightning the devil is spanking his wife.

Okay, I have no idea where these saying came from but they helped my interest in capturing lightning. Before I figured out how to actually photograph it I tried seeing it and snapping a picture. It didn't work. I was always to slow; camera was pointing the wrong direction, and ISO (film speed was wrong). Bottom line - I had no idea what I was doing. I'm not a real good "read the directions" person. Seems I'd rather waste a lot of time and energy trying to figure things out myself. Know anyone like me?

Truth is I didn't learn by reading how. I was with some other photographers and one was talking about how to photograph lightning.

He said something like: you need a tripod, a cable release, put your camera on the tripod, tightening it in place, look through the view, find the horizon or where the lightning is, put your camera on "bulb" which opens your lends, twist open the cable release and watch the show.

Duh!

The trick of making sure you're capturing lightning comes with time and tested experience. As you play with it you'll learn to pay more attention to the horizon so you can get the full effect of the experience. It's a point of reference so to speak. Without the horizon all you'll get is sky and lightning. If that's all you want that's great. Do your thing...that's the most important creative avenue.

Resurrection came about one stormy night, lots of lightning, in a small West Texas town. On the northwest side of town there was large field with a massive pile of oil field pipe. Metal pipes are magnets for lightning. There I stood, camera on a tripod, cable release attached to my camera, camera on bulb, lens open and miles of West Texas in my view.

The show had already started and I was pumped. What a night this was going to be. I had even brought a diet coke, something to snack on, and enthusiasm.

I stayed and took photo after photo. Taking some photos for a strike or two and some for minutes of strikes. My experience is when you're basically on flat ground, which describes this part of West Texas, taller than most of the surroundings, and lightning is all about you. It'll come to you.

The lightning storm was splitting and coming my way, from both directions.

Hint - time to leave.

But no, I saw power lines on the horizon and knew I had to try and capture them and the lightning. I reset my tripod, found the horizon, camera on bulb, twist open the cable release and WOW. A five, yes 5, minute exposure sounded about right. Not smart, but about right.

Second hint – again, time to leave.

More experience has taught me that when you smell sulphur, you should have left.

The lightning storm was splitting and moving my direction and I smelled sulphur, but "OH" what a photo that would be if I could capture it. Finally grabbing all my equipment and the little bit of common sense I had left I made a mad dash for my pickup.

Did I get the photo? Had no idea, this was way before digital. I took the slide film ninety miles to be developed. Two hours later, my slides where ready, and I couldn't wait to look at them. Thirty-five slides later.... there it was.

I had it!

> "God made the light, I just paint with it."
>
> \- Anonymous

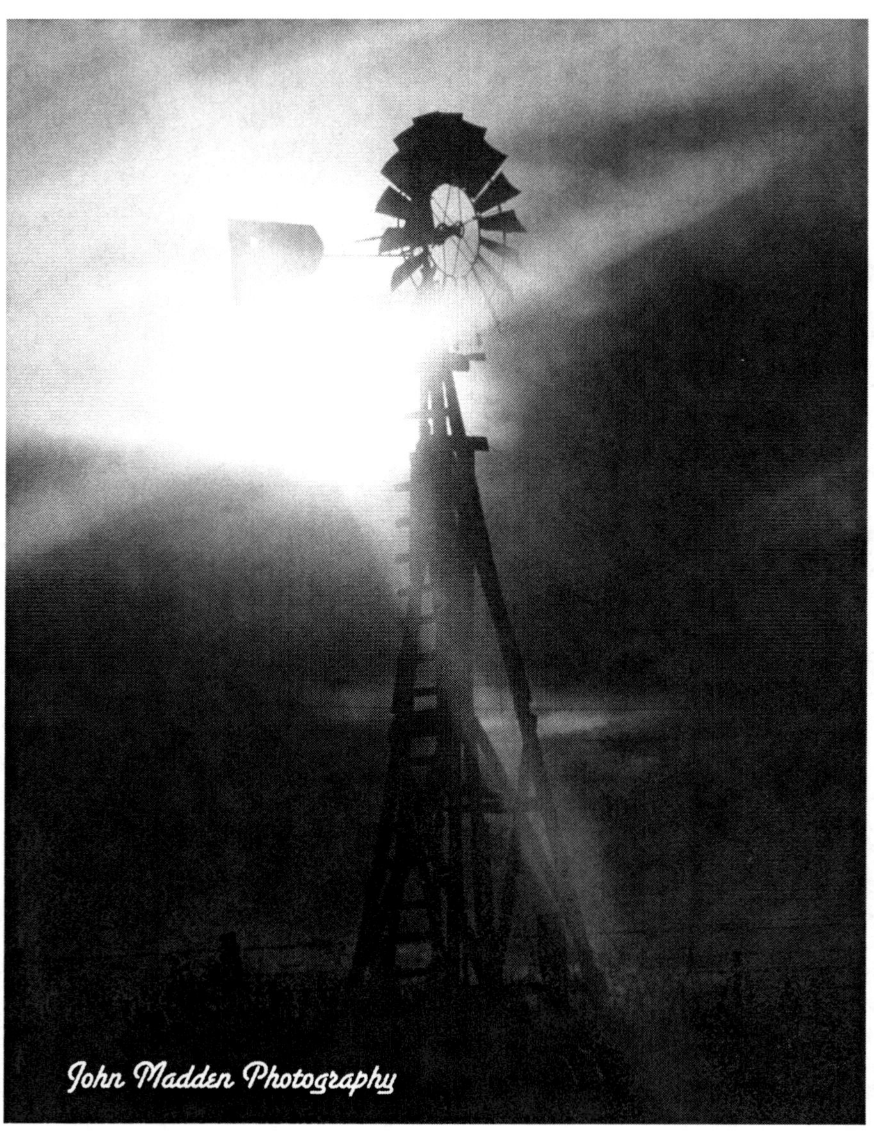
John Madden Photography

Easter Morn

This photo was given to me during a very difficult time in my life.

My high school sweetheart, my wife and life of twenty- one years and I had divorced. Our children were with her at her parents and family, all of whom I loved with all my heart.

I was alone, it was Easter and I needed something to help me feel better if not somewhat good about myself. I picked up my camera and went in search of a photo. I needed to be creative. I needed to feel the excitement and joy I feel when my camera becomes my eyes. I drove around the little West Texas town I lived in and knew I needed to explore the county for windmills

Northeast of town, I drove in and around pump- jacks, caliche roads, ruts, across cattle guards to finally find this old windmill. It stood on the western horizon; it reached out and drew me to it. The sun was playing hide- n- seek with the dark clouds, but I thought I would have a chance to get the shot.

I got out of my pickup, walked towards the windmill, put my camera up to my eye and all of sudden the clouds engulfed the sun and darkness covered the sky. I stood around, walked around and waited for such a long time, hoping the sun would come out. It didn't.

The day was my life at the time, dark and without direction. I was so full of pain; I dropped to my knees and cried. All of a sudden I felt a tap on my right shoulder, I tuned around to see who was behind me. No one was there, but a few cattle watching me and wondering what I was doing on such a cold, bleak, and dark day.

I heard a voice, saying, and "turn around, look up" and as I did the sun broke through the clouds.

My camera appeared before me, my right eye looked through the viewer, my right hand hit the trigger and it captured three or 4 photos. In a matter of minutes clouds re- captured the sun and darkness covered the landscape.

This photo is the gift I was given. I stayed on my knees, cried tears of joy and said a prayer of thanks.

Please accept this gift, this photo from my Lord and Savior as a reminder that he is always with us, he always hears our prayers, to have faith and to be ready for life.

> "Sometimes I do get to places just when God's ready to have somebody click the shutter."
>
> - Ansel Adams

CHAPTER 7

In Honor

I come from a Military background, Dad was in the Air Force, I was in the New Mexico National Guard and US Army, over fifty percent of Madden's have been in the military, 2 received the Congressional Medal of Honor in the Civil War, one was in and wounded at the Battle of Little Big Horn with Lt. Col. George Custer, 13 died in Vietnam, 1 in The Twin Towers, 1 in Afghanistan, and 1 in Iraq. So far this is all I know, however I continue to search for more records.

I proudly fly an American flag in front of my house honoring "All gave some and some gave all." I'm American proud and I have no prejudice except those who are prejudice. My family comes from Ireland, Scotland, England, African Americans, Australia, and Native Americans and it doesn't come much more diverse that.

I honor all first responders and all who stand their watch for the security, health, and freedom that we have in our country as well as all countries.

Charlie was an uncle who served in WWII who I greatly admired, liked and, respected.

The 10th Anniversary of the Wall was a gift that came as a result of a friend's invitation, Jim Goss, to come to the Wall. It was a very emotional experience but worth it.

"137 years later, Memorial Day remains one of America's most cherished patriotic observances. The spirit of this day has not changed - it remains a day to honor those who died defending our freedom and democracy."

- Doc Hastings

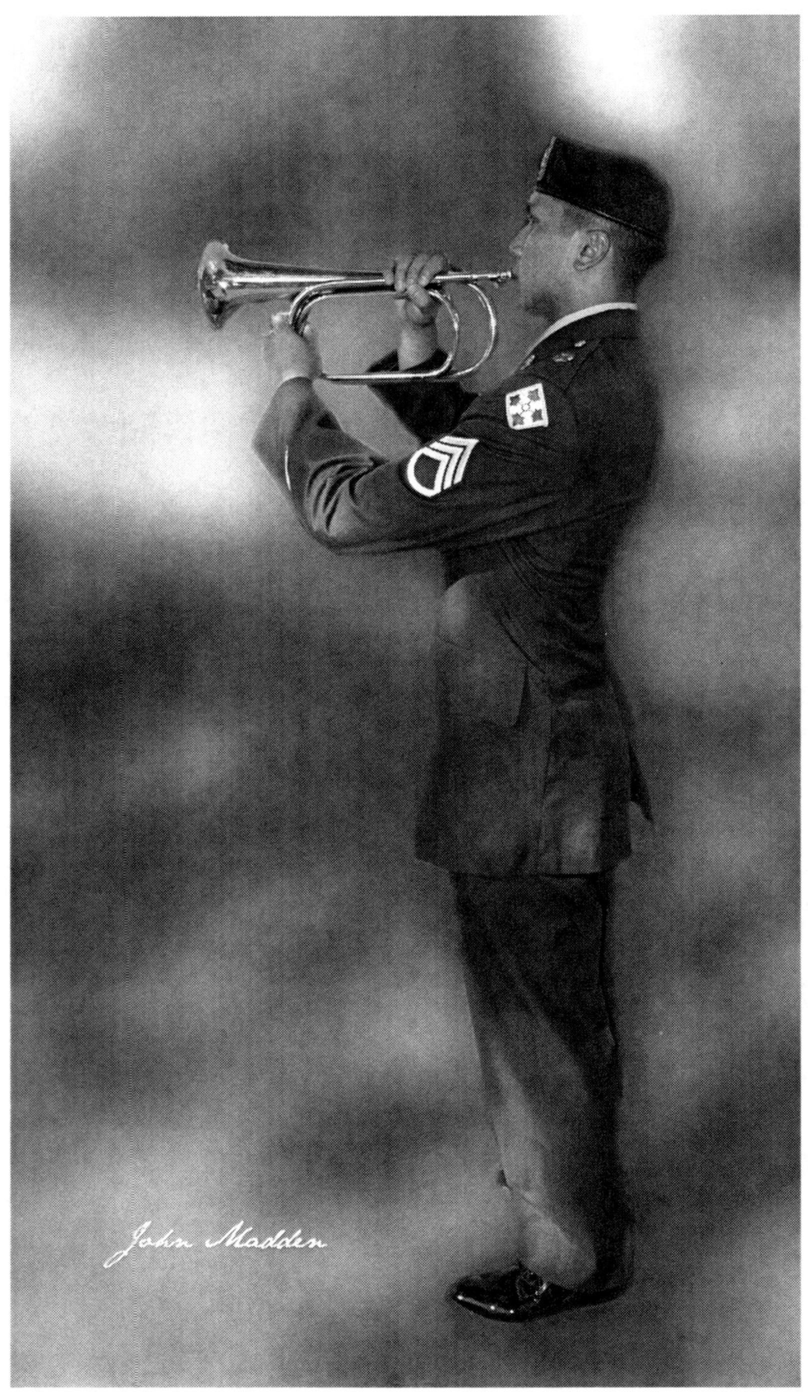
John Madden

Charlie WWII

He was a cowboy's cowboy who outlived the 'Ole West. The ranching, bronco busting, working pre- dawn to past sunset, never backing down, standing up for what's right no matter the cost kind of cowboy. This was back when friendship was often the only constant, riding for the brand (doing what was needed for whomever you worked for) and Saturday night's entertainment more often than not was a friendly barroom brawl.

No killings, just good ole last man standing fights, then beers all around.

He was a commo (communications) man for General George Patton during the big one. He spoke highly of the "Ole Man", as he called him. Would have followed him anywhere, in fact he did, all over Europe. His troops nicknamed him "Old Blood and Guts."

Interesting facts from Charlie; Patton's first combat was against Poncho Villa along the US- Mexico border, his troops fought in Sicily, France, and the Battle of the Bulge. Charlie was with him during the Battle of the Bulge laying commo lines.

Patton also represented the US in the 1912 Stockholm Olympics in the pentathlon. He was in five events: running, swimming, fencing, riding, and shooting. Shooting was his poorest event, but he still placed fifth.

Charlie was a man's man like Patton. Proud, hard worker, dependable, dedicated, a friend forever when he knew you. Born poor he had several businesses when he joined Patton upstairs. Mostly he was American Proud to the core.

It was an honor to know him, to be called a friend and have the privilege of sitting with him as he told story after story. He was a cowboy, solider, business owner, father, grandfather and full time BS'er.

He wasn't what I'd called a "flower" person, but I think he'd appreciated the simple flower arrangement that was his diligent honor guard on his last roundup.

"I look forward to a great future for America - a future in which our country will match its military strength with our moral restraint, its wealth with our wisdom, its power with our purpose."

- John F. Kennedy

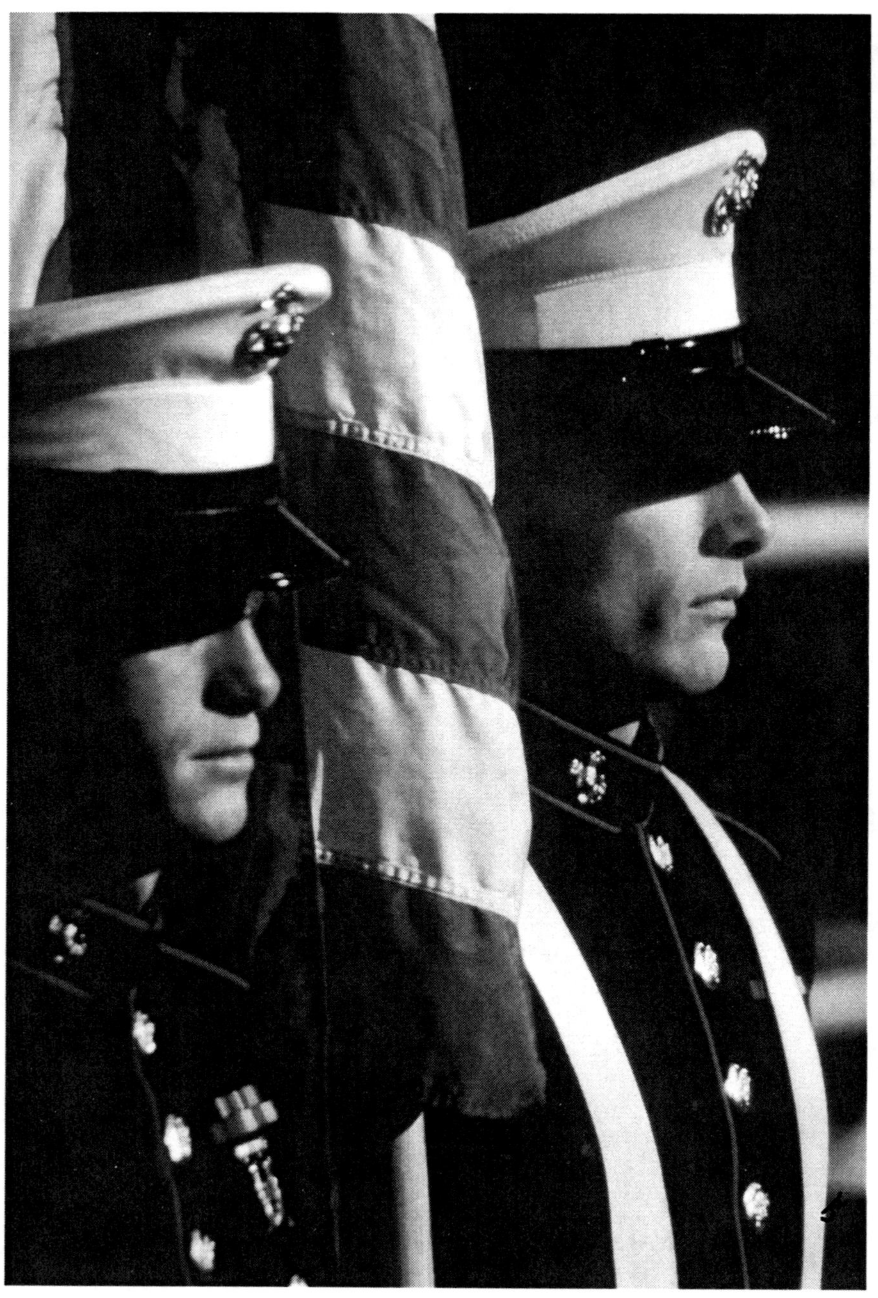

10th Anniversary of the Wall

Jim Goss, a fellow and very talented photographer, Vietnam Veteran and new friend from the Vietnam Memorial Day gathering at Angel Fire, New Mexico had invited me to the anniversary. He worked and still works there as a volunteer for the National Parks Service. His stories of the emotions, pain, suffering, healing, drama, and photographic opportunities drew me in like bait to an award winning trout.

Flying in from West Texas I saw a mixture of travelers, but not many identified as soldiers. That was a carry over from the lack of support and caring from the Vietnam War and protesters. No parades, welcome home banners, recognition for doing what they were ordered to, trained, to do or their suffering.

They were told not to wear their uniforms, change into civvies (civilian clothes), and not to tell anyone they were Vietnam Vets. They were the scum of the earth. Baby killers. Their average age was twenty- two. The average age off a combat soldier was 19. Draft age was 19- 25. Training was hard, short, and difficult, without a lot of help once bullets started flying their way. Early on they learned, "a bullet doesn't care who you are."

Being shot at wasn't personal and nighttime was death time.

They left the world (United States- home) to go to a place people wanted to kill them for nothing other than they were American soldiers.

- Vietnam War, also known as the second Indochina War - 1954 to 1975
- 1st American soldier killed July 8. 1959: last April 29, 1975

- 8 women's names are on the Wall- all NURSES
- 245 received the Congressional Medal of Honor
- 58,178 total American casualties

Going to the Wall went from okay, no, why, can I do this, should I do this, it's to expensive, will take up work and vacation time, to I just have to do this. I'm an AFB (Air Force Brat- Dad was in the Air Force); I was in the National Guard and US Army. A photographer with a feeling of deep responsibility to go in honor of friends and all who gave their all and those names on The Wall.

Nothing can prepare you for The Wall. Nothing!

It's in an elongated V shape. The names start on one end, as one, and as the Wall expands in width and height more names are added to a pentacle center then sloping downward to one again. It's beautiful, at the same time calming, reverent, humbling, and patriotically simple.

The first day was a blur and I couldn't concentrate or focus on taking pictures. It was so overwhelming and emotional. I couldn't even get my camera bag out of Jim's trunk. All I remember was this feeling of being off balance with a fading vision of someone circling around me, as I walked, stumbled, stopped, cried, and felt the spirit of the Wall and every name on it. That was Jim.

I truly felt as if hands were holding me up and directing me up and down the length of the Wall. Tears erupted down my checks, emotions ran through my being like bolts of lighten, my breath came in shuttered gasps, and I was dysfunctional.

The next day there was a reading of the 58,178 names. Talk about an overloaded emotional roller coaster with nothing but ninety-degree ups and downs. My saving grace was I was able to put my camera to my eye and with stealth zoom in to capture people and moments.

As the readings continued I saw two Marines standing, off to the right side of the podium, at attention, strong, confident, proud, sharp and holding two American flags.

Wow! They were a gift from the spirits of those on the Wall.

I honor those who made the ultimate sacrifice by giving away more photos than I've sold. It came about to be shared and given away.

That's my job and why I took the photo. Besides I had no choice!

> Get off your butt and join the Marines!
>
> - John Wayne

Every Book has a Last Page and this is Mine!

"Stories never really end...even if the books like to pretend they do. Stories always go on. They don't end on the last page, any more than they begin on the first page."

— Cornelia Funke, *Inkspell*

Be a part of the photo not just the photographer.

- John Madden

I hope you enjoyed this, maybe got some ideas, but mostly go out with your camera, in cell phone or real one, and have FUN! Find out what's out there that you haven't seen before.

Keep an eye out for the next book **'Through My Eyes – The Art of Faces."**

In the love of photography and their stories,

John Madden

CPSIA information can be obtained
at www.ICGtesting.com
Printed in the USA
FSOW02n0941160915
11138FS